SAI BABA: A RAY FROM THE SUPREME

To

Bhagwan Sri Sathya Sai Baba
Who is the way, the destination and
The Ray Supreme, with deep
devotion, reverence, love and
infinite craving

SAI BABA

A RAY FROM THE SUPREME

KRISHNA NANDAN SINHA

ABHINAV PUBLICATIONS

abhinav publications

First Published in India 1997

Publishers

Shakti Malik
Abhinav Publications
E-37 Hauz Khas
New Delhi-110016

ISBN 81-7017-349-3

Lasertypeset by

Tara Chand Sons
Naraina
New Delhi

Printed at

D.K. Fine Art Press Pvt. Ltd.
Ashok Vihar
Delhi

CONTENTS

PREFACE

At a time when Sai literature has attained mountainous proportions and the Sai movement all the world over has reached its very apex and crown, promising the beginning of a new spiritual era and the return of the golden age, how does one justify the writing of yet another book about Sai Baba? Verily, the writing of books about Sai Baba has assumed the status of a minor industry. But it is an industry which is probably well past the point of maximum returns, but the quality of its subject is fortunately such that it will continue to engage the attention of brilliant intellectuals and writers who may also be seekers in the realm of spirit. This is one reason why I have attempted to write yet another book on Sai Baba. But there are more reasons for doing so.

Raja Rao, the eminent Indian English novelist, while discussing his aesthetic has asserted, time and again, that writing for him was a *sadhana.* His masterpiece, *The Serpent and the Rope,* is truly a quest novel, the author's spiritual odyssey. Ramaswami, the chief protagonist of the novel, deeply embedded in Indian culture and spirituality, finally receives illumination and moves towards the *still centre* when he finds his guru. In his other novel, *Cat and Shakespeare,* metaphysical complexities make room for the simple and compulsive concept of total surrender. It seems to me that writing is not only something one does for love, it is also a sure and certain way of achieving illumination. It is a spiritual exercise costing not less than everything.

In my Foreword to *Sai Baba: The Rose-Fire of Heaven,* I have stated the simple rationale behind the book:

> Divine love, in reality, does not inflate one's ego; it simply prompts one to get immersed in its central reality for further union and deeper communion with God...

Thus I planned to write the second volume with the express intention of making it objective and more or less impersonal, not to talk about myself or give vent to my ego and sense of self-importance. Whereas, the first volume, *Sri Sathya Sai Baba: Absolute Sole Lord of Life and Death,* is as much about Baba as about myself and my family, the second one is centred on the emergent principle of divinity incarnated in the figure of Sai Baba, his *mahimas* and glory, his message of *Sathya, Dharma, Love,* peace and *Ahimsa.* So, while writing these books I have surrendered myself wholly to the work to be done. Pen in hand, I have contemplated with the familiar patterns of meditation the divine form of Baba and He, in turn, it seemed, had taken my pen in his hand and had allowed my perceptions to bloom like so many fragrant jasmine petals and made me write with his sheer, bare penetrating power. And the rest is not my business.

However, writing these books has been a kind of *Sadhana,* the spiritual exercise of a very high order. I have experienced the supreme bliss of a lifetime's death in love, ardour and selflessness and self-surrender. Another obvious reason for attempting to write a third volume is the natural and legitimate desire to complete the trilogy and live up to the saying that God is infinite; and his tale, his splendour, power, glory and mystery are likewise infinite and interminable. I also believe in the beautiful verse of George Herbert, the greatest devotional poet of the seventeenth century, who said in his famous Jordan poem: 'There is in Love, a sweetness ready penn'd/ Copy only that and save expense.'

It may be fair to mention that I have eschewed symbols and metaphors for poety in this third volume. In the first volume 'Love, thou art absolute Sole Lord of Life and Death', the first line of the seventeenth century Metaphysical poet, Richard Crashaw's *Hymn to Saint Teresa,* provides the title of the book and features as the central metaphor of the book. In the second volume, *Sai Baba: The Rose-Fire of Heaven,* the structural symbolism is from great medieval Italian poet, Dante who envisions God as a single flame in which all the scattered leaves of the universe are bound together in one volume so that what one speaks of is a single flame. And of course, the single flame and multifoliate rose have been derived from the same source and from T.S. Eliot's *Four Quartets*: 'The Fire and the rose are one.'

For the purposes of this volume, there is greater accent on plain statement rather than on esoteric or traditional symbolism, imagery and metaphor. This is not to suggest, by any means or manner, that the author has taken a holiday from poetry or that he has suffered a surfeit, excessive surfeit of poetry. Far from it! Poetry is and has been the corner-stone of my vision, As we know there are two kinds of poets: those who write verses and transmute their experiences, feelings and visions by finding the apt metaphors for poetry. And there are those who do not write verses, but are gifted with more than organic poetic sensibility. It is their prerogative to see as the poet sees; the simple in its strange and rich complexity, and the complex in its tantalizing simplicity. My professors in the American University where I was working towards my degree of Doctor of Philosophy in English literature, used to tell me that often I mess up the meanings by my reflections on art and literature whereas the ideal condition for a writer of doctoral dissertation is to write in a tangible and concrete manner and style with copious evidence from the texts so as to make the thesis logical and acceptable. I did not realize the wisdom and sanity of this advice and comment at that time, but now having mellowed to some sort of maturity and ripeness, I have come to realize that poetry can sometimes become an enchantress, a fatal Cleopatra to obscure the meaning and the reality and it can be an entirely unnecessary and undesirable superstructure. However, the poetic orientation has been integral with my mental make-up and temperament and I cannot altogether silence the true voice of my feeling. But the style employed in this volume acquires its transparency and glow from a close adherence to plain facts. Whatever poetry there is, has to do with the subject matter. Since God is the greatest poet, the creator of the vast cosmos, He is the poet *par excellence.*

Enumerating the reasons for writing the third volume about Sai Baba, I must mention some personal reasons and compulsions as well. In the year 1973 when I was first initiated into the life of spirit, baked in the white heat on burning wheel of fire, the fire of seething torment and suffering, I started worshipping Sai Baba and placed his pictures in the shrine. Immediately, mysterious manifestations started occurring day in and day out. These were the visiting cards of God in the form of *vibhuti, kumkum,* and turmeric *amrit* on the pictures and large footprints on the floor accompanied with automatic lighting of fluorescent tubes in the shrine and the heavenly aroma and fragrance of jasmines in the atmosphere. Later automatic messages began to appear on pieces of paper at regular intervals. In one such message scribbled in green ink, there was a clear injunction to me to write a book on Sai Baba in the manner of my great well-wisher and benefactor, late Professor Vinayak Krishna Gokak. Since I was with Sai Baba largely unfamiliar and had little preparation or mental equipment to venture to write a book on him, I did not take the injunction with any amount of seriousness. Time passed and I went on living and partly living, suffering the slings of outrageous fortune and repaying the debt of my *karma* in my past lives. Then by the strange logic of circumstances, I was drawn to the auspicious and redemptive orbit of Sai Baba and felt the stirrings of a new consciousness and embarked on the inward journey to discover the God within. It was then that Swami's tangible, concrete presence was felt in my life and my life exfoliated like unfolding lotus in the radiant light of the sun. Many boons were granted to me and my family and I landed at Prashanthi Nilayam in 1985 as Professor of English at the Sathya Sai Institute of Higher Learning. At the same time, my spiritual odyssey continued.

It was in 1987 that I experienced a climactic rendezvous with that fell sergeant Death and was face to face with oblivion. It was then that Bhagwan Sri Sathya Sai Baba came to the sick-room as a saviour. He blessed me with affirmations and declared explicitly with abundance of love that he was very happy with me and my work. He granted me a fresh lease of life as it were, and reminded me that I had still lot of work to do for Him. I had absolutely no idea what kind of work I could do for him, specially with my state of health with residual effects of paralysis. All through my life I had been a teacher in colleges and universities and had kept myself engaged in the life-long romance with words. So, with Baba's blessings and grace, I decided that the only meaningful work that I could do for him was to write books on him and sing the glory of the Eternal Absolute that has incarnated in flesh and blood as Sri Sathya Sai Baba. Since I cannot teach or do any active service with this frail and ageing body, but my mind, with the grace of Swami, is still resilient and full of prowess and insights. Now that I have completed the trilogy, I feel like one who revels in the cherished bliss of completing one's mission. I have the greatest and everlasting sense of fulfilment that I have been a humble instrument in divine hands to do the task assigned to me and, like John Milton, I can say with deep satisfaction: 'They also serve who stand and wait!' 'If the readers who will read the trilogy and find themselves any closer to the understanding of Sai Baba and his *avataric* mission and have a clear perception of being, awareness and bliss, I shall consider myself to be extremely fortunate and think that my labour has not gone in vain.

Finally, I may like to add that seeing the face of God or an *avatar* who has assumed a tangible concrete presence in an age when the dimensions of faith, hope and love seem to have been lost, is the greatest thing that can happen to anyone, and to sing the glory of the eternal Absolute incarnated in human form is sheer ecstasy, the very consummation of consecration and devotion to the divine. May this be the destiny and destination of all spiritual seekers.

Krishna Nandan Sinha

1

THE LIGHT FROM ABOVE

Sri Sathya Sai Baba has, on several occasions, made certain pronouncements about himself which not only clarify the nature and mystery of his divine advent, but also deepen the mystery a thousand fold and leave us wondering if he is the Eternal Absolute, the one God or *sarvadevata swarup* who has descended on earth like Rama, Krishna, Jesus Christ and Buddha, in the fullness of an *avatar* to lead mankind to discover divinity and attain self-realization or *mukti* or liberation. One of his epoch-making declarations is contained in his statement during the world conference of Sri Sathya Sai Seva organization in Bombay on May 17, 1968 'Why I incarnate?' and 'My Reality'. He has given a firm, concrete and tangible expression of his advent and mission as an *avatar*. The announcements and their contents are too well known to require a fresh recital. On another occasion he has said: 'I am infinite, I am immeasurable, I am unique, I am incomparable. Equal to myself, I am my own measure, witness and authority.' And further he states his true identity when he says: 'I am the *Satashya Sathyam,* the Truth of truths. Why has truth come on earth in human form? To plant in the heart of man the yearning for Truth, to place man on the road to Truth, to help man to reach Truth by loving instruction and by the final gift of illumination.'

These are truly gems of pronouncements made by the *avatar* which are self-sufficient, autonomous and complete and can hardly be glossed over. But the problem is how can the finite, the limited human entity, understand the infinite, unique and incomparable Godhead? Baba says:

> You cannot understand my reality either today or even after thousands of years of austerity or inquiry, even if all mankind

> join in that effort. But, very soon, you will be aware of the bliss showered by the divine principle, which has taken upon itself this body and this name.
>
> (Sathya Sai Baba)

And he declares his unity with every sentient thing in the universe and his identity as the one God:

> I am not Sathya Sai Baba. This is the name by which you know me today. All names are mine. I am the one God who answers the prayers that rise in human hearts in all languages from all hands, addressed to all forms of deity.

Sri Sathya Sai Baba has come from the beyond, the high heavens above to pitch his tent on this temporal and time-bound earth of ceaseless flux and change in order to restore India and the world to its spiritual glory and carry the message of spirituality through the evangel of love, truth, peace and *ahimsa*. He further says that the labours of the avatar in his mission will not fail and in the end of this manifestation, the earth's age will begin anew and the golden years return. Many who believe in Baba believe in the divine pledge and its certainty and inevitability. Professor V.K. Gokak has put it very nicely and in emphatic terms when he says:

> I am one of those who believe in him and the surety of his pledge. The question may be asked: why? On what grounds? My one answer to that question is: I believe in Baba and the surety of his pledge, not because I am what I am, but because Baba is what he is.
>
> (V.K. Gokak, *Sai Baba: Man and Avatar*, p. 75)

It follows from this that it is all a question of faith and belief. If one believes in the divinity of Baba or has experienced it at first hand, all doubts and questionings end and it becomes a lot easier to surrender to Baba as the ultimate and supreme reality. Still the crux of the problem remains in this age of rank scepticism, crass materialism and lost dimension of religion to develop the supreme continence of affirmation that helps one recognize the indwelling God in one's heart. It is through the process of devotion and continual meditation that light dawns upon one's consciousness and faith breaks in life. The name and thought of God is the lantern that illuminates the dark recesses of the heart and soul and leads one to the summit of the hill from where the resplendent face of God is seen.

Commonly speaking, the concept of incarnation is a difficult metaphysical formulation which is familiar mostly to the East, that too in Hindu religion. Lord Krishna has said to Prince Arjuna in the battle-field at Kurukshetra:

> Every time virtue wanes in the world and vice and injustice are victorious, I become visible and thus I appear from age to age for the salvation of the righteous, the destruction of the wicked and the re-establishment of virtue.
>
> (Krishna, Srimad Bhagwat Gita)

And Sri Sathya Sai Baba echoes the same truth when he says:

> For the protection of the virtuous, for the destruction of evil-doers and for the establishment of righteousness on a firm footing, I incarnate from age to age. Whenever *ashanthi* or disharmony overwhelms the world, the Lord will incarnate in human form to establish the modes of earning *prashanthi* (peace) and to re-educate the human community in the paths of peace.
>
> At the present time, strife and discord have robbed peace and unity from the family, the school, the community, the society, villages, the cities and the state. The arrival of the Lord is also anxiously awaited by saints and sages. Sadhus prayed and I have come. My main tasks are fostering of the Vedas and fostering of the devotees. Your virtue, your self-control, your detachment, your faith, your steadfastness, these are the signs by which people read of my glory.
>
> (Sathya Sai Baba, 'Why I incarnate?', *Sai Baba and His Message,* ed. S.P. Rahula *et al.,* p. 13)

The one-to-one correspondence between what Krishna meant and what Sai Baba means is very surprising indeed. For the first time nearly five thousand years after the time of Krishna's death on February 20, 3102 B.C. when *Kaliyuga* commenced that Sri Sathya Sai Baba has appeared as a *poorna avatar*. It is not possible for human beings to grasp the full significance of the descent of an *avatar* in the phenomenal world for guiding individuals and societies towards spiritual regeneration.

Although much has been written about the concept of the *avatar,* there is still a good deal of confusion, incoherence and doubt about the manifestation of the ultimate and eternal Absolute in human form at crucial and critical junctures of human civilization and history. Whereas in the perennial religions of the East specially *sanatan dharma* and the Hindu and Buddhistic thought and tradition, it is accepted as essential and natural phenomenon for the maintenance and preservation of the moral and spiritual order of the universe and the laws of the cosmos. The eternal laws of nature, the revolution of constellation, the dance of the elements, the cycle of seasons, time and flux are sustained by divine will and the direct manifestation of the supreme Godhead in phenomenal world. As Professor Gokak has rightly observed,

> But these laws of Nature can be transcended whenever a ray, direct from the Supreme penetrates the universe. This ray is power, will, thought and feeling combined in a solar flash. The Word which is at the very root of creation, is a complex seed symphony of Truth, Beauty, Goodness, Love, Delight and Power...When does the Ray descend? As the Gita says, whenever righteousness is at a low ebb and the unrighteous ride on the crest of the wave, the Ray takes the human form to establish the reign of Truth again, to protect the good and punish the wicked.
>
> (V.K. Gokak, *Sai Baba: Man and Avatar*)

At this stage, it may be fair to have an idea of the ultimate Absolute that chooses out of his own Will to descend as a Ray from the reservoir of cosmic power and energy and take on a temporary habitation on earth. It is the destiny of mankind, the individual souls and *atma* to merge in the universal *atma* either through *jnana* (flawless knowledge) or through meditation or intense *bhakti* (devotion) leading to total surrender and identification with the Supreme Lord who is both formless and with tangible form. Who is this Supreme Being? All round we see everything in a state of flux and change. Behind these everchanging phenomena there must be a permanent base as the changes cannot take place in a changing background. The

सत्य
प्रेम

permanent base also must be something eternal. The stars, planets and elements follow various rules which must ultimately be unified and controlled by some power. This is an eternal and omnipresent power. The ancient *rishis* called it as *sat.* It must have some purpose and must be leading the universe to some goal and consciously direct the universe. So, another aspect of this principle would be the consciousness of everything past, present and future. This the *rishis* called *cit.* We all recognize suffering and pain as essential part of the human condition and yearn for *ananda* or joy continually. Unless the eternal Absolute itself is bliss unalloyed, it cannot lead others towards bliss. Thus, we can infer that the supreme principle is *sat* (pure existence), *cit* (pure consciousness) and *ananda* (absolute bliss). This is all information that the sages and seers of the past have handed down to us about God or the Eternal Absolute.

How does one relate oneself to the eternal absolute who is *satchidananda*—Being, Awareness and Bliss. The devotion of the *bhakta* does not merely confer boons affecting material life; it can also compel the formless Godhead to manifest itself. In the words of C. Balasingham,

> The supreme divine power is present everywhere, very much like gravity, as the invisible supporter and controller of the manifested universe. The various shrines are like substations connected to a vast power grid and we can tap the divine power from any substation. The nature and extent of the use of that power depends on the individual—his preparedness and state of development. Where the devotee prays to the Supreme earnestly in a particular form for a direct vision, God manifests himself in that particular form.
>
> (C. Balasingham, *Sai Baba and the Hindu Theory of Evolution,* p. 53)

Thus the idea of a personal God is very convenient and helpful for the purposes of pointed, intense and total concentration on God in a particular name and form.

In addition to transient manifestations of the Eternal Absolute for brief periods, we also have *avatars* or manifestations lasting several years, when God walks the earth in human form.

Says Mr. Balasingham,

> The Avatar is only a convenient focus for the operation of the divine power in a human and tangible way. There have been several *avatars* in the past. Krishna, Christ...Buddha are really a few that come readily to mind. In our times, we have divinity living and moving with us in human form as Bhagwan Sathya Sai Baba.
>
> (Balasingham, *Sai Baba and the Hindu Theory of Evolution,* p. 53)

Balasingham goes on to say:

> When we say God or divinity is walking the earth in human form, what exactly do we mean? We have seen that Absolute or divinity is vast power that which envelops, permeates and controls the universe, if we imagine the Absolute as a vast power grid then Bhagwan Sathya Sai Baba is a substation from which that power flows and operates in a visible form. The physical body of Bhagwan Baba is only an instrument through which divine power operates. The real Sai Baba is this power and this is the one to which he refers when he uses the word I. Baba himself made a distinction between his body and his power on the Christmas day in 1970: 'My body like all other bodies is a temporary habitation; but my Power is eternal, all-pervasive and ever dominant.'
>
> (C. Balasingham, *op. cit.,* p. 54)

Explaining the point further, Balasingham says:

> The relationship between the general divine power and this substation needs elucidation. In the first place, there is no exclusiveness; there were, are and will continue to be, other substations through which this vast power of the Absolute operates. Lourdes, for instance, continues to be a place where miraculous cures occur even after Bhagwan Sathya Sai Baba started his miraculous cures. The difference is that in Lourdes there is no visible source, no tangible output through which the power operates. On the other hand, Sai Baba is a visible, moving, talking substation...Everyone of us, according to Hindu philosophy, is a focal point of this Absolute consciousness. It may be asked what is the difference between

> us and Sai Baba? In him the power flows out unhindered and with full force and power. In us that power is almost completely muted.
>
> (*Ibid.*, p. 55)

This is a good and plausible explanation of the manifestation of the divine in human form. Since each one of us is the spark of the same eternal Absolute, the divine power which is muffled and snuffed out in oneself on account of the veil of *maya* and ignorance of the real self, has to be realized through constant and continual *sadhana*.

Returning to the image of the light or the Ray from the Supreme, the eternal sunbeam, we find it to be the most appropriate and functional imagery for the definition of God. Most religious poets have used the imagery of sunlight, the elemental sunbeam, to express what is inexpressible. Dante in the last canto of *The Divine Comedy* describes his feeling of supreme bliss and ineffable ecstasy when he sees the ultimate reality as a single flame. The light and fire imagery occurs with great frequency in *Four Quartets* of T.S. Eliot, culminating in the last section of *Little Gidding*: 'The fire and the rose are one.' In the works of all mystic poets, Vaughan, Rumi and others, the obsessive imagery is that of light. In the holy Bible, light is described as the synonym of God. The descent of the divine principle on earth is like the coming of the transcendent sunbeam to scatter the darkness and gloom on our planet. Sri Sathya Sai Baba himself says:

> Generally, an *avatar* is described as coming down from a higher status to a lower one. But no, when the baby in the cradle weeps, wails and clamours for help, the mother stoops and takes it over in her arms. Her stoop is not described as coming down.
>
> (*Sathya Sai Speaks,* 10, p. 229)

When asked by a devotee if the idea of descent of God on earth and the ascent of man to God are different, Baba replied that both are the same. The one for whom the light descends would inevitably move from darkness to light, from falsehood to truth, from mortality to immortality. The light in this sense is redemptive, a sure means of taking mankind to the path of self-realization.

Apart from being the transcendent eternal sunbeam, an *avatar* is sweetness and light. In the words of Professor Gokak,

> The *avatar* moves like a Colossus among men. The past, present and future lie open to his gaze. What is more, he has the power of grace. An avatar has sixteen *kalas* or phases. Five of these he shares with human beings — the five doors of perception—sight, hearing, smell, touch and taste. Another four he shares with human beings—mind, heart, intelligence, *turyavastha* or transcendence of intuitive experience. The seven phases that follow are characteristic of a *poornavatar*, an integral *avatar*: grace, Anugrah or special grace, the power to create a new order of life in society, new states of consciousness in individuals or new objects, the power to support and sustain what is inherently good, which may happen to be defenceless, the power to destroy what is evil...The Divine itself is a supreme paradox. He is the One in the many, Spirit and Matter at the same time. Himself transcendental, the divine has become the universe itself. He is Infinity which can crowd itself into a little room. Immortality itself; it is also Death. He is both Time and Eternity. He is Love, but this Love is red in tooth and claw. Formless, yet the divine is father of all forms.
>
> (V.K. Gokak, *op. cit.*, pp. 17-18)

An Avatar has the four essential attributes of Godhead — omniscience, omnipresence, omnipotence and omnifelicity. Thus an *avatar* comes to usher in a new age for humanity and take mankind along the path of self-realization and evolution of consciousness.

Sri Sathya Sai, like Krishna, is a full *Avatar* with all the sixteen *kalas.* He is also the *Avatar* of Love and Truth who has come in order to light the camp of Love and Truth—a light from above, perfected in the triumphant symbol of Love. Baba prescribes the way in which the Avatar can be used by mankind:

> The way in which an *Avatar* is used for one's liberation and uplift is: watch his every step, observe his actions and activities, follow the guiding principle of which his life is an elaboration. Mark his love, his compassion, his wisdom; try

to bring them into your own life.

(*Sathya Sai Speaks*, 6, pp. 166-67)

As for the avowed role of Sri Sathya Sai Baba, he has, time and again, reiterated his purpose in no uncertain terms. Long time ago, Lord Krishna came to foster the forces of peace and love and he had to use the surgery of war in order to safeguard the *dharmic* way of life. The battle of Kurukshetra removed the cancer threatening to wipe out righteousness, peace and harmony as a powerful and aggressive military caste had grown arrogant and aggressive. To put an end to their tyranny and flagrant violation of justice and right action, the Lord himself offered to become the charioteer of Arjuna, the Pandava prince. And when Arjuna the mighty warrior and archer and Krishna the eternal charioteer worked together in unison, there was nothing that could not be achieved. All this happened in the *Dwapar yuga*. Even before that in the *Tretha yuga,* Lord Rama was forced to fight the demons and the demon king Ravana who symbolized the unrighteous way of life.

In the present age, when we are living in an age of crisis, at the edge of a precipice and a nuclear doom looks so very close and distinctly in the realm of possibility, one may ask what kind of surgery would Sai Baba take resort to. He says: 'There is a cancer in the body which must be removed.' The world is the body of God. Sai Baba who has descended as light from above proposes to employ a gentler therapy for the purpose. In other words, can the power of light dispel the black pall and scatter the darkening gloom? In his famous interview with John Hislop, R.K. Karanjia and a few others, Baba has categorically assured that the present *avatar* had come to prevent such a catastrophe. He has further said that there will not be general or all-pervasive world war though there might be small wars or skirmishes here and there. He even told Howard Murphet, if the Governments stood in the way, the Governments would have to be changed. During the past decade, the end of the cold war between the two power blocs and agreements about nuclear disarmament are proofs enough, if proofs are needed, that the *Avatar* has kept his promise. Baba has also very succinctly prophesied that early in the next century, the promised millennium or spiritual regeneration will get under way and become a living reality. Baba uses a different metaphor when he says, 'White ants are in the tree again. In ancient times, the tree was cut down. Now we try to save it.' This is another instance of the Lord's infinite compassion and love for humanity. Baba's another crucial declaration is:

> I have come in order to repair the ancient highway, leading man to God. Become sincere, skilful engineers, overseers and workmen, and join me...and I have come to sow the seeds of faith, of religion. I have come in response to prayers of sages, saints and seekers for the restoration of *dharma.*

Thus, the authenticity of Sri Sathya Sai Baba as the 'lawn of blue light', to use a phrase from a poem by Professor Gokak, seems to be hundred per cent true. Millions in India and in far-away countries regard him as a major *avatar*. What is more, many regard him as an incarnation of Love, Truth and Purity. Now the impression is growing fast in Christian countries that Baba is Jesus Christ come again as prophesied by none other than Christ himself. Most often, he is regarded as an *avatar* of *Shiva Sakti,* that is, the male and feminine aspect of Godhead. This has gained credence mainly because Sai Baba himself chose to reveal the reality of a myth and a legend concerning sage Bhardwaj. And then there is evidence of Sri Sathya Sai Baba's complete identification as an *avatar* of that mendicant *fakir* who lived at Shirdi, Maharashtra, and is believed to be the incarnation of Shiva. The third Sai *Avatar* according to Baba's own testimony and enforced by the boon given to sage Bhardwaj that Sakti would incarnate as Prema Sai in the state of Karnataka after Sri Sathya Sai Baba attains *mahasamadhi* at the age of ninety-six. So every available evidence supplements the view that Sri Sathya Sai Baba is the Ray from the Supreme come to fulfil his self-chosen *Avataric* role and that the whole humanity would bathe itself in the effulgence of his love.

When the ray from the divine, absolute centre descends on earth, it sheds its lustre and glory the way it likes that suits his overall plan and mission. Since it is the coming down of light from above it has no restriction. It is in itself a free agent, omnipresent and omnipotent always and at all times. Sri Sathya Sai Baba has said that he has incarnated as a human being in response to the prayer of saints and sages. He has further elaborated:

> I have chosen my mother. This is the prerogative of an *avatar* to choose his parents. The mother is the recipient of the first grace of the divine principle. The father earns the privilege, name and fame for being the father. For ordinary human beings, the parentage, place and region of birth is predetermined by the *karma,* merits and demerits of past lives.

Then, there is the difficult and obtuse question of what is called immaculate conception. If the *avatar* takes human birth out of his own volition or *sankalpa,* the normal biological and genetic laws of biology or procreation do not hold good. In the immortal epic *The Ramayan,* it is mentioned that Vishnu or Narayan decided to incarnate on earth in response to the plaints and prayers of saints and sages and assured them that he would live on earth for *vishwakalyan* or the good of the world and humanity. After making this declaration, he started thinking where to incarnate and ultimately, choosing King Dasrath as his father, he appeared as Rama, the eldest son of the king. Rama knew that he was not only the offspring of an earthly king, but also the omnipotent, universal, the one without a second, creator, preserver and destroyer, the eternal Absolute. In the case of Lord Krishna also, the *sankalpa* or the resolve to manifest in human form was voluntary. Moved by the great sorrow of the mother earth and her wailing lament as also by the steep decline and eclipse of *dharma* Narayan manifested himself as Krishna, the full *avatar* for the protection of the good and the virtuous and destruction of the evil. He was born to Devaki, the consort of Basudeva, after she had given birth to seven offsprings, all of them were killed, one after the other, by the demon king Kansha.

All we can say is that the advent of an *avatar* is outside the purview of all logic or the known material laws of nature. Sri Sathya Sai Baba has said that he alone is the symbol of all those incarnations who have manifested in time. He represents the

Hindu Trinity of Brahma, Vishnu and Mahesh, the quintessence of all divinity.

The advent of Lord Buddha is an exemplar of supranormal and miraculous manifestation. Before incarnating the divine principle latent in him resolved: 'I would take birth as an offspring of a Chandrabanshi Kshatriya family whose kingdom is in the snow-covered regions of the Himalayas. Queen Mahamaya, the consort of king Shuddodhana, dreamt on the night of her confinement that a constellation which was resplendent and shining, of the colour of a rose-pearl sailed in the night sky, stationed on a milk-pure white elephant and subtly entered her bosom and prince Siddartha fashioned his body right there like a full-blown moon and appeared on the earth as an *avatar*.

The example of the advent of Jesus Christ fully supports the theory of immaculate conception and divine birth. Gabriel, an angel sent by the Heavens, appeared before Mary who was betrothed to Joseph of the tribe of David. The angel told Mary not to worry or fear over anything because she has already received the grace of God. The angel further told her that she would conceive soon and give birth to a son who will be called Jesus. Mary, very upset over the news, voiced her apprehension, 'How could this be possible? I do not know any man.' 'Do not harbour such thoughts. You will be ravished by the Holy Ghost himself and you will give birth to a holy child who will be described as the son of God.'

Ramkrishna Paramhansa who had revealed to his closest disciple, Narendra or Vivekananda that the absolute Ishwar who had appeared as Rama and Krishna has now incarnated and his tangible concrete presence could be visualised in him. Ramkrishna Paramhansa had chosen his mother and place of birth. Khudiram Bhattacharya, who is known as the father of Ramkrishna, gained the distinction of being the father of Ramkrishna only in name. While visiting a temple at Gaya where he had gone to offer *pind-dan* to his ancestors, he saw a dream and heard a voice from the sky telling him that Narayan will be born in his family and offer him the proud privilege of being called the father of an *avatar*. Since Khudiram Bhattacharya had already attained three score years, he prayed to the powers that be: 'Both my house and my heart are too modest and small to house the Lord of the universe.' But the voice of the oracle proved true. When Khudiram Bhattacharya reached home the first thing his wife Chandramani Devi told him was that while he had gone to the temple for *darshan,* she experienced a strange phenomenon: a luminous, bright and resplendent ray entered her bosom and filled her with infinite joy and spread through every vein and bloodstream and plunged her in perpetual ecstasy.

Finally, the advent of Sri Sathya Sai Baba on earth as *poornavatar* conforms to the self-same pattern and we have the evidence of none other than the chosen mother of the *avatar,* Ishwaramma. N. Kasturi records:

> One evening Swami was sitting in a circle, surrounded by some close devotees. One of the devotees was a scholar conversant with the knowledge of *Shastras* and *Purans.* He put a plain and direct question: 'Swami, was your birth a delivery or an entry?' Everyone was stunned by the question. But Swami, turning towards Ishwaramma, said, 'Tell Ram Sharma what happened on that day near the well where you had gone even after being cautioned by your mother-in-law.' Ishwaramma said, 'My mother-in-law has had a dream in which she saw Sathya Narayan in very clear and concrete visualization. She warned me not to move about in the village. On that day when I was near the well to fetch water, I saw a dazzling column of light in the sky moving fast in the direction where I was. It seemed to me as though the moving column of that celestial light gracefully entered my bosom.' Swami cast his glance over the bewildered face of Sri Ram Sharma, smiled serenely and said: 'This is the answer to your question. My advent was not delivery in the normal sense of the term. It was an entrance.'
>
> (N. Kasturi, *Ishwaramma,* Hindi edn., pp. 33-34)

All this substantiates the view that the advent of an *avatar* defies all logic and notions of cause and effect, conception and developing embryo, confinement and delivery. It is a mystique, a supranatural event and rightly so, because the divine principle, the ultimate Absolute decides to incarnate from time to time. The light from above dawns on earth and assumes the form of a full-blown lotus. The advent of the *avatar* is an epochal event of great significance and it is suffused with mystery and awe. When the Lord decides to incarnate and walk the earth for the fulfilment of the mission to redeem mankind, he takes on the splendour and the beauty of both the human and divine essence which is his nature. Sri Sathya Sai Baba has pointed out clearly:

> Since I move about with you, eat like you and talk with you, you are deluded into belief that this is just an instance of common humanity. Be warned against this mistake. I am also deluding you by my talking with you, by engaging myself in activities with you. But, any moment, my divinity may reveal itself to you. You have to be ready, prepared for the moment. Since the divine is enveloped by humaneness you must endeavour to overcome *maya* that hides it from your eyes.
>
> (Sathya Sai Baba: My Reality, *Garland of 108 Precious Gems,* ed. N. Kasturi, p. ii)

We can say in conclusion with a fair amount of certainty that the advent of the Divine principle has the element of the supernatural, the mysterious and the miraculous which the limited and finite consciousness of man cannot comprehend. Perhaps such a state of consciousness is described by T.S. Eliot in his poem *Gerontion* where the feeling of religious awe is transmitted through one of the richest and most evocative symbols of Christ, the tiger, who comes after the present withering of values in a calamitous age, suggesting spiritual regeneration:

> Signs are taken for wonders, we would see a sign,
> The word within Word, unable to speak a word
> Swaddled with darkness, in the juvescence of the year
> Came Christ the tiger.

At another place in *Burnt Norton,* the same poet attempts an imaginative and emotional reconstruction of the state of beatitude associated with the rising of the lotus in the dry concrete pool filled with water out of sunlight from which the lotus rose quietly. The lotus obviously stands for Vishnu incarnating himself. This is a consummated symbol of the act of creation itself. This special configuration suggests the permanence of the timeless reality.

So, Sri Sathya Sai Baba is the ray serene, the light, the blazing knot of fire merged into his personality. Baba himself puts it admirably when he says:

> No one can understand my mystery. The best thing you can do is to get immersed into it. There is no use arguing about pros and cons; dive and know the depth, eat and know the taste. Then you can discuss me to your heart's content. Develop truth and love and then you need not even pray to be granted this and that. Everything will be added unto you unasked.
>
> (Sathya Sai Baba)

2

THE LIGHT THAT NEVER WAS ON LAND AND SEA

We have seen how Sri Sathya Sai Baba is a substation of the vast power grid and operates effectively and continually from that centre. Since he relates himself directly to the still centre, and is the prime mover of creation and the entire cosmos, this power is universal and eternal. He stands at the junction of the human and the divine and emanates the redemptive beam of light that never was on land and sea. In earlier centuries, the light celestial had descended on our planet earth and shed its lustre and brilliance for the purposes of ushering in the golden age and for the redemption and salvation of the human lot. This transcendental, all powerful column of light was representative of the past *avatars* like Rama, Krishna, Jesus Christ, Buddha and many other partial *avatars* who walked the Earth from time to time. They came to the earth and assumed human form just for the sheer love of humanity. They have belonged to the class of liberated and enlightened souls whose earthly sojourn has not been for paying any *karmic* debt, but for teaching the less fortunate souls and offering them the recipe for better and more fruitful, moral codes of living.

In the words of Vivekananda,

> Higher and higher than all ordinary ones are another set of teachers, the *Avatars* of Ishwar, They are Teachers of all teachers the highest manifestations of God.
>
> (Swami Vivekananda)

The concept of Incarnation is integral with Hindu religious thought and with Mahayan Buddhism. Even in Christianity, Jesus of Nazareth is believed to be the one and only manifestation of divine power, the son of God, the Holy ghost who trod the dust of Palestine and subsequently emerged as the supreme principle of divinity. One has only to study the Holy Bible to garner information about the power, splendour and glory of Jesus Christ. His teachings, based on love, faith, hope and charity and his commandments, specially the ones delivered to his disciples in his Sermon on the Mount speak volumes about his wisdom. The chief and unique power of an *Avatar* consists in his power to change the very spirit of the age and to bring about a wholesale transformation of the minds and hearts of men. All the *Avatars* have displayed this power in abundance. Since the light has come from above, it is just in its nature to illuminate the dark corners of the world as well as the dark recesses of the human heart.

Talking about the *Avatars* Annie Besant, the great theosophist thinker, has stated that the treasure trove of perennial philosophy and wisdom of *sanatan dharma* is buried in India; but in the modern age of science and easy communication, the entire wisdom has been properly disseminated and has even become the spiritual heritage of all mankind, irrespective of caste, creed, religion or nationality. No wonder that the Vedas, Upanishads, the *shastras, purans* and Bhagwad Gita, not to speak of the vast Sai literature are works within the reach of the entire humanity which aspires to explore the realm of spirit. The very fact that Bhagwan Sri Sathya Sai is now not only a familiar name in the West and all over the continents of Australia, Europe. America, Africa, but millions worship him as their personal God. It may be noted that never before in the long history of *Avatars*, such a phenomenon had been witnessed. When Rama and Krishna started their great *avataric* mission, very few people realized the import of their work or cared to follow their teachings. It was only in the case of Lord Buddha that a substantial part of the world accepted him as a great teacher. But at the present moment of mass communication, global travel in the jet age and international channels of printing, time and space have ceased to matter and a large number of seekers pay their obeisance at the lotus feet of Sai Baba and experience his divinity at first hand and without any shadow of doubt.

It is in this sense that I have given the caption 'The Light that never was on land and sea' to this chapter. Many devotees living thousands of miles away from Baba have direct experience of miracles, visions, directions in dreams, accumulation of *vibhuti* on pictures in their worship room, and they are drawn to the *Avatar* as files of iron are drawn towards a very powerful magnet. Containing the translucent beams of light, Baba manifests that light wherever he pleases and the result is universal adoration of his power and mystery as omnipresent, omniscient and omnipotent God. Indeed, he truly represents that light which never was on land and sea. In the age of Romantic revival, the poets longed to see this light, but the waves of industrialism and scientific materialism obscured their vision, and they thought if there was no God they would invent one and found in Nature a substitute for divinity, a light that never was on land or sea. The primacy of spirit over matter and the transcendence of consciousness over reality permeates the thought of the nineteenth century German philosophers and of the British poet and thinker, Samuel Taylor Coleridge. One notices a close proximity between these thoughts and the ancient perennial wisdom of the Indian scriptures.

When the Ray Supreme chooses to penetrate the universe, there is illumination and *only illumination*. It is not that a cosmic firework is witnessed. All that happens is that no area of human consciousness is left in the dark to languish in sempiternal gloom. A new and altogether welcome synthesis between subject and object is established and the distinction between *being* and *becoming* is obliterated. The light that engulfs the universe may either appear as both personal and impersonal. It may either take the form of a Krishna or Sai Baba. In its impersonal aspect, the light may be universal light, the naked majesty of the sun and the stars. In the eleventh chapter of *Srimad Bhagwat Gita* the vision of the divine in its total beauty, splendour and terror was bestowed to Arjuna. We are aware of the glimpse of the eternal and ultimate reality vouchsafed by the *avatar* to the intimate and fortunate ones who were held near and dear to the *avatar*. The child Krishna opened his mouth in order to show Yashoda, his foster mother that he had not eaten the mud. And Yashoda, on her part, saw both creation and dissolution going on in that flash of vision, universes rolling within the narrow confines of the *avatar's* mouth. Lord Krishna also showed his cosmic form at the time he admonished Prince Arjuna to cure him of his feeling of wavering and disaffection and his recoil from action in the battle-field. When we glance through the biography of Sai Baba of Shirdi we find that as a child, while playing with marble with a neighbour lad he won all the marble counters. The neighbour boy brought the *lingam* from the shrine of his mother and played with it and lost it to Babu, as Shirdi Babu was called. When the mother of the neighbour boy came to know of it, she rushed to the spot where the boys were playing and entreated Babu to return the marble *lingam*. Babu denied having taken the *lingam*. On being asked to open his mouth, he did so. The pious lady saw universes rolling in the mouth of Babu and lay prostrate at his feet. She had the advantage of the divine vision. In the biography of Sri Sathya Sai Baba, entitled *Sathyam, Sivam, Sundaram* we read that Baba showed the images of all the *avatars* to his mother Ishwaramma and some close devotees. It is reported that the images were produced in reflections on water, and many of the onlookers could not withstand the impact of that sight and even fainted. It only proves the point that humankind cannot bear very much reality.

Howard Murphet, in his beautiful book *Where the Road Ends,* says:

> You will appreciate the truth of the statement that the only difference between a full *Avatar* and the omnipresent, omniscient, omnipotent God without form is that the *Avatar* has a name and a form. These, while making him more readily available to mankind, do not limit the amplitude of his divinity. Seeing him in the form of a man, the human mind is inclined to question these three fundamental facets of Almighty God. I have often heard him say that there is only one God and He is omnipresent. Can this small man in red be omnipresent? Can he be everywhere at once? The mind questions. Yes, he is everywhere in spirit, the Holy Spirit. Many of his close devotees perceive him around them all the time, often as Light. But, then, when he deems it necessary, that Light will suddenly take subtle form of Sai

Baba. This I know personally from experience.

(Howard Murphet, *Where the Road Ends*, p. 198)

Furthermore, Howard Murphet affirms the supreme continence of his affirmation *vis-a-vis* the divine principle manifested in Sai Baba as Light. He records:

> Now, after many wonderful years of benign influence of my shining star Sai Baba, I have no doubt whatever about his omnipresence, his omniscience and its relation to his omnipotence...I have no doubt that he will call to himself, at the right time all those who are ready to take a step forward into the Divine Light and become his helpers. Thus, in ways that we cannot yet foresee, he will carry out his divine mission for the enlightenment of the whole world, creating a new epoch for mankind. Yet, after the partial insights into the mission of the *Avatar* I find that God remains a great mystery.

(Howard Murphet, *Where the Road Ends*, p. 199)

Answering to a question by John Hislop about pointed concentration on the form of God, Sri Sathya Sai Baba says:

> The best *sadhana* is that every act through the day be done as worship of God. God is like the electric power. Heart is the light bulb. The wiring is the discipline. The switch is the intelligence. Just turn the switch and there is light.

(John Hislop, *Conversations*)

John Hislop describes how Sri Sathya Sai Baba answers to his question in respect of the divinity and universal omnipresence of Swami.

> H.: Swami, here just now we actually witnessed a part of this amazing story. How can this all be? Swami holds the entire universe in His Hand. He bears the responsibility for the inconceivably immense entire universe. And how can he at the same time give this detailed attention to the lives of individual devotees?

> Sai: It is as you say. Swami holds the universe in His hand. But devotees learn of the glory and majesty through Swami's

attention to each one, personally. That Swami holds the universe, yet at the same time fully cares for the lives of his devotees even to the smallest detail is the measure of His glory that the devotee can understand.

(John Hislop, *Conversations*, p. 173)

That Bhagwan Sri Sathya Sai is the translucent, all-pervasive Light that never was on land or sea in recent times after the dawn of *kaliyuga* nearly five thousand centuries ago cannot be called in question. We have not only the concrete and irrefutable evidence of astrology, Sai Baba's birth chart at the time of his nativity, the opinion of experts in reading the aura surrounding the faces of eminent human personalities, but also the personal testament of devotees.

Most of these evidences have been discussed at some length in the author's earlier volume, *Sai Baba: The Rose-Fire of Heaven*. However, a brief resume may be given here for the sake of coherence and continuity. The first evidence is that of the ancient *Jyotish Shastra* enumerating the principles of astrology. The position of the ascendant in the *lagna,* the nakshatras and other major planets or constellations at the nativity time of the subject is supposed to be very crucial and significant in determining the life and character of the subject. The study of the birth chart of Sri Sathya Sai Baba reveals the nature and quality of his divine descent. Born in *Akshaya* Kartik when as many as four powerful planets were staying in conjunction in the ascendant. The combination of Sun, Saturn, Venus and Mercury indicated beyond any shadow of doubt the advent of a *Maha Purush,* a great being or an *avatar* was born as the very quintessence of Light and Love in order to herald a golden era for humanity. The advent of the Sai *Avatar* had been prophesied thousands of years ago in the Upanishads as also in *Bhrigu Samhita, Nadi* documents scribbled on palm leaves by ancient sages and seers and in *Satcharitragrantham,* the repository of ancient wisdom. These priceless records describe the divine attributes of Sai Baba whose principal task is *dharma paripalan, paropkar* and *bhakta samrakshan.* He has *laghima, anima* and *mahimas,* the power to shower grace and splendour. He is omnipresent, omniscient and omnipotent. It is also predicted that his powers would increase tenfold at the time of *pralaya,* calamity and dissolution. He will show himself at many places as column of light and perform many divine manifestations like keeping an airplane airborne without petrol. Finally, it is mentioned that he will unfurl a *dharma dhwaza* after the completion of his *avataric* mission at Whitefield, Bangalore. It is difficult for us to disbelieve all these predictions. From the recorded evidence of so many miraculous manifestations of the omnipresence and omniscience of Baba and his Christ-like power of resurrecting the dead, multiplying the quantity of food etc., one is inclined to believe in the divine advent of Sai Baba.

However, the greatest achievement of Sai Baba is to turn people Godward and plant in the human hearts the seed of faith and impregnate those hearts with the elixir of pure, selfless love and thus bring about the transformation of hearts.

Another stong evidence of Baba's divinity comes from an entirely different source—Frank Varoneshky, a professor at the University of Arizona, U.S.A., who has earned the distinction of being an undisputed expert in the study of the halo or aura that surrounds the faces of individuals. He has the privilege of studying the aura on the faces of eminent individuals in all walks of life. According to him, the attendant aura speaks volumes about the character and personality of the subject. Whereas the aura round the faces of ordinary mortals is, more or less, non-descript, null and void, the aura encircling the face of a superhuman person or an *avatar* is expansive and its lustre extends up to the sky which is limitless. Professor Varoneshky was bewildered and enthralled to see the aura round the face of Sai Baba. According to him, it was a white and pink aura of the colour of love. This aura became golden like sun and turned into blue colour which is the colour of love when the *bhajans* were being sung. Professor Varoneshky suggests that this aura signified the boundless energy of love and he has no hesitation in saying that aurawise Bhagwan Sri Sathya Sai was God, the diamond-like brilliance of his eyes expressing the unfathomable depth of his love.

The personal experiences of many a devotee richly substantiate this aspect of Sai Baba, the dramatic operative principle of his divinity manifested as a Ray from the Supreme.

The present author himself experienced the surge of waves and waves of unearthly light emanating from the eyes of Sri Sathya Sai Baba on that fateful day of summer, 1973 as he stood face to face with Baba in an attic room by the side of the interview room. It was not only ecstasy, but also sublimity that filled the vessel of his being. The author still recapitulates that moment of epiphany, akin to the intersection time when one is very near illumination and experiences the process of being burnt out.

An American devotee Jack Scher records his intimate experience of his first encounter with Sai Baba in images of poetry. He says:

> One personal *leela* was my discovery that during *bhajans* I could close my eyes and suddenly the whole scene I had been watching turned into beautiful shades of intense rose, pink, mauve and orange. At first I thought it was an after image but the scene kept changing. The audience would fade and I'd see huge palaces with gigantic walls and turrets. When Baba came outside, I could close my eyes and the whole scene would turn into a soft and yet vivid pink. He lit the sky with his presence.
>
> (John Scher, 'Can God Hear Me?', *Transformation of the Heart*, ed. Judy Warner, p. 7)

We are aware that in some of the materializations, specially photographs and cards, there is the imprint of three words — T.P.S.—Howard Murphet records in one of his books, *Sai Baba: Avatara.* Baba answered his query and explained the fact that T.P.S. was his trade mark. It meant Tara Parthi Sai. We can conjecture that it also might mean Tara Patri Sai and Tara Prema Sai. The direct apocalyptic experience of Pauline Kirby is strange and unique as she visualizes the descent of a star on the Good Friday day of 1977 that transformed her life and left an indelible imprint on her mind. That is how she describes the descending of the Holy Spirit from the Sky as Sri Sathya Sai Baba:

> After spending a very lovely evening in attunement...with God and Nature, I retired to my room. It just so happened that this particular room had a skylight so I could look up

and gaze at the star-lit sky...I looked up at the skylight; and suddenly a star started coming down from the heavens. It streaked across the sky getting brighter and brighter and continued right on through the window, entering directly into my room. It was awesome. I was utterly stunned and amazed...Almost instantaneously my room shone with a very strong light. Everything seemed so clear and beautiful. It was totally overpowering. I was in a complete state of awe and wonderment. I remember saying, 'Is this happening to me? Is this a dream? Am I asleep?' But I was totally awake and my mind was perfectly clear. Yes, it was really happening...The star then began to flash various streams of light, and all these flashed before my eyes, I heard a very loving voice giving me clear directions about my life. The messages were very simple, and there was no doubt in my mind that this was guidance from above...The voice also told me to become a vegetarian, become celibate, and begin to worship God. Later when I came to Sai Baba, I realized that these were his exact teachings...The star stayed with me for quite some time. The flashes of light and the voice all happened in a very synchronized pattern, like an orchestra playing a symphony around the cosmic dance of life...yes, I realized there is really a God, and he is directing every move of my life...Sometime during the star's presence, I remember feeling very afraid, and immediately the image of climbing up and downstairs came into my mind. To me, go down meant to descend into darkness and the unknown, while to go up meant to follow the light and to know what the real Truth is. I now realize how similar this insight was to *Asatoma* prayer of Sai devotees: Lead me from the unreal to the real; lead me from darkness to light; lead me from death to immortality. Even then, Baba was imparting one of his essential teachings. Soon I started reading about Sathya Sai Baba and the very first book, *Vision of the Divine,* disclosed Swami's trade mark, T.P.S. It means Tara (Star), Puttaparthi in the form of Sathya. Then I realized it was he who had come as that wonderful star; it was he who had descended into my world on Good Friday night; it was he who had completely changed my life.

(Pauline Kirby, 'Descending of the Holy Spirit', *Transformation of the Heart*, ed. Judy Warner, pp. 79-83)

Thus, it is clear from the vivid and authentic experience of Pauline Kirby that she, like William Wordsworth, had the intimations of immortality on the night of Good Friday which transformed her life and brought her into the orbit of Sri Sathya Sai Baba and nearly made her an apostle of Christ. She may not be Paul, but her name has the implicit suggestion of its derivation from the name of the great apostle. The star symbol is extremely relevant in this context. It encloses within it the power, majesty and brilliance of that perpetual star which God is.

It may also be noted that the account of Pauline Kirby, describing the descent of the Holy Spirit, is essentially poetic. Verily it is through poetic perception and imagination that such a tenuous experience as the vision of the divine can be grasped and communicated. In this connection, one is tempted to quote the poem of Professor V.K. Gokak a noted Kannad and Indian English poet in which he envisions Sai Baba as 'a lawn of blue light'.

Baba is a lawn of blue light
With a May-flower on top of his hair
And a golden lily on his cranium.
He is the healer of a world in pain,
The blue-throated God
That drinks the poison of its suffering
To make it happy and whole.

This blue-throated God is also the Sun-crystal as described in V.K. Gokak's another beautiful poem:

He sits in the sun in the meridian hour of exceeding glory. And the sun is mellow to his eyes and limbs,
The scion of the sun becomes a sun crystal.
He receives the quintessential ray and concentrates it on the world that it may be purged of its dross.
And in the moment of Apocalypse, that sun-crystal
Melts into the sun.

(V.K. Gokak, 'Scion of the Sun', *op. cit.*, p. 84)

One can say, in conclusion, that Sri Sathya Sai Baba is the perpetual star that becomes multifoliate rose so as to make humanity aware of his divine reality. He appears as light or the single flame that burns continually to take the entire humanity upward to the path of illumination making us aware of the God who resides within us. Baba's divine power is the power of spirit and his light is the sempiternal light that shines everywhere. In the words of Professor Gokak, Baba's power is something that descends from the thousand-petalled lotus, the elemental exercise of a will that is omniscient and omnipresent. It is the will that sees and acts simultaneously. What it wills fills and fulfils itself in space and time. But it bides its time, unwarped by slushy sentiments, unbiassed by impatient hurry. And when it strikes, it is for all to see, like a column of light that unites the earth and sky.

Professor Gokak describes some of the external, breath-taking and almost unbelievable phenomena that go by the name of miracles, signs and wonders:

> It is the cascade of *vibuthi* or holy ash, endless, exhaustless. It is the crystallization of *lingam* after *lingam,* spheroids of alabaster or jade from the silk soft leaves in the abdomen. It is the ceaseless oozing of honey from the heart of granite itself. It is the descent of a succession of golden images of gods and goddesses—from nowhere. It is the transformation of stray particles of sand on a sea shore into the divine image of Sri Krishna, the reconstitution of water into petrol. It is the profuse inpouring of *vibuthi* and the massing in of *kumkum* behind the glass framed on the photograph, the footprints in holy ashes leading to the worship room in a house or out of it. It is flower moving marvellously from the top of a photograph to its base, or whole garlands aflutter...It is the rain that suddenly stops raining or the electric bulb that blazes with light when the whole area is plunged in darkness. It is the shaft of light that hits you in the eye from a photograph.
>
> (V.K. Gokak, *op. cit.,* pp. 71-72)

That Sri Sathya Sai Baba is divinity incarnate, the *logos,* the

Word or the supreme Brahman is no longer debated or doubted. As time passes, the absolute certainty and authenticity of his incarnation or *avatarhood* is becoming as clear as daylight. Even those who consider Sri Sathya Sai Baba merely as a holy man and saint *par excellence* are veering round to the view that he may be representing the absolute and ultimate reality, the *still centre* which is the source and spring of all light and knowledge. Howard Murphet in his book, *Where the Road Ends,* makes a mention of the prophecy of Sri Aurobindo about the victory day:

> The noble work of Sri Aurobindo did, however, have its Victory day. This day still celebrated in his *ashram* was on the 24th November, 1926. His followers believed that Sri Aurobindo had been working for years to bring about what he called Krishna consciousness on earth. On that day he announced that his goal had been achieved. Krishna consciousness had come on earth and so this was his Victory day. On the day before this announcement, that is, on the 23rd November, 1926, *Avatar* Sai Baba was born. A large number of his followers including myself see him as *Avatar* Krishna born again.
>
> (Howard Murphet, *op. cit.*, p. 245)

Dr. Samuel Sandweiss, a renowned American psychiatrist, was drawn towards Sri Sathya Sai Baba and delved deep into the reality of the *avatar* and he was able to apprehend the ultimate reality of Baba. He records:

> Good news about the presence of Sai Baba among us will spread quickly throughout the world, I am sure—even though as he says, it will take a while for us to comprehend his full significance or the meaning of his message. It has been my good fortune to draw close to him at a time when it is still possible to become friendly with him on a personal level and see the clear signs of his greatness in a close and intimate way. Yet I feel that soon Baba will become but an orange speck on the horizon, surrounded by millions of eager faces. And like the people in his village who were once blessed to know the sweetness of his being from daily personal contact with him, I too will one day be saddened

by having to view him only from a distance. But it is enough to know that Sai Baba exists at all. I feel deeply fortunate to be able to play a part, in some small measure, through this book in an evolutionary phenomenon moving inexorably towards realization: world consciousness awakening to its own glorious potential, and to the presence of a being who may indeed be ushering in a golden age.

(Samuel Sandweiss, *Sai Baba: The Holy Man and the Psychiatrist,* p. 231)

The experience of Swami Abhedananda, a close devotee of Sri Raman Mharshi, who achieved a high level of spiritual development through *sadhana* and longed to see the divine in human form, is very revealing. One morning at 4 A.M. he had a vision of both. Raman Mharshi and Sai Baba. The figure of Sai Baba underwent a metamorphosis and it seemed to Swami Abhedananda that Sri Krishna was standing before him in his tangible concrete presence. Even John Hislop in his wonderful book, *My Baba and I,* has related his experience of a drive with Baba on his car...when he was amazed and wonder-struck to see the attractive shades of deep blue on the face of Baba. He could not help asking Baba: 'what did that colour actually mean?' Baba was quick to respond: 'It was the colour and complexion of Krishna.' It may be interesting to sort out the revealing experiences of devotees, specially their initial and final perceptions of and insights into the nature of the *Avatar*. The most common thing is that the hearts and souls of persons ready to receive spiritual initiation are instantly lit up by the light of Baba's divine presence.

Sri Sathya Sai Baba is a cosmic visitor, an *avatar* of Light and Love and his glory and splendour cannot be diminished by censure or criticism by cynics, ignorant and hollow men without faith. Baba simply brushes aside or ignores such criticism by saying that he feels sorry for those persons who hardly know either him or themselves. In his famous interview granted to Mr. R.K. Karanjia of *Blitz* Magazine he has answered all his queries and convinced Mr. Karanjia of his divinity. Mr. R.K. Karanjia, a progressive thinker and committed Marxist, has beautifully summed up his overall impression of Sri Sathya Sai Baba and his mission. He has put it on record and has become an ardent devotee of Baba:

> What finally is the sum of Sathya Sai Baba's mission? God realization through self-realization, he answered. In his series of interviews, Baba has shown the Godward path to the realization of *sat-chit-ananda,* that is, experience, knowledge and bliss absolute. According to Baba, this highest state of consciousness or enlightenment is possible for every man and woman to achieve once he or she is liberated from the ego-bondage of body and mind to realize the true self—that is *jivatma. Jivatma* is the abode of the indwelling God in man. It is the embodied essence of *parmatma,* the Cosmic Spirit. The *Avatar*'s mission, according to Baba, is to help mankind dissolve the barrier of the ego and the mind with it so that the embodied *jivatma* can merge and fuse with the universal *Parmatma,* the mighty ocean of nectar divine as he describes it, to raise mankind to a race of good men and good women. Baba seeks to resolve the universal problem of man's alienation from man, God and nature with the Sai philosophy of pure spiritual love. Sathya Sai Baba provides the desired formula for escape from the terror of existence. Only evolution to a higher plane of consciousness can save man from this terror, this darkness and cold, this frozen spiritual misery.
>
> (Samuel Sandweiss, *Spirit and the Mind,* p. 255)

Mr. Janardan Thakur, another important journalist and feature writer of *Sunday,* has also published his interview with Baba. He had gone there in a critical and sceptical frame of mind, harbouring doubts about not only Baba's power but also his gown, his hair. Baba was generous and compassionate enough to allow him to examine the gown and the hair and he reports that there could not be a wig; it was a head full of hairs. Similarly, when reputed para psychologists and a bunch of psychiatrists visited Prashanthi Nilayam Baba accepted them with grace and removed all their doubts. This author also remembers the time when Baba passed along the line of the teaching staff and mumbled sadly, 'You all are doubting Thomases.' Baba has said on many occasions, 'If you say yes, I also say yes, yes, yes. If you say 'no', I also say no, no, no.' What is of crucial importance is the attitude of total affirmation, faith and unswerving belief in the existence of God. Since the individual *atma* is basically an *ansha* or part of the *paramatma* according to Vedanta, the eternal Absolute having created the universe at its own pleasure, the One having become many, there is hardly any separation. 'Thou art that' is the basic and central truth. That is what Sri Sathya Sai Baba means when he says that God realization is self-realization.

Verily, Sri Sathya Sai Baba is the unique and incomparable source of Light, a regal and imperial Lighthouse, the blazing fire in the midst of a black pall to point the way to the pilgrims assailed by fancy lights and enchantments. To change the metaphor, he may also be described as that sempiternal erosionless rock in the bosom of the sea, the ocean of *sansar*. In the dark and stormy weather it is merely a sea-mark, helping the mariner to cruise safely on to his destination; but in calm and tranquil weather, it is what it always was, the symbol of permanence. Waves wash over it, the sunlight caresses it and the sea wind blows over it, but it is always firm and erosionless. In this world of constant flux Sai Baba is the only unchanging Absolute who sheds his light on each and every fragment of the phenomenal world, the Light that never was on land or sea. He is at the spring and the source, the root and the foliage of every sentient thing, specially mankind, for it is man who has the privilege of evolving to higher and still higher states of consciousness.

Howard Murphet in the last chapter of his book, *Where the Road Ends*, speaks of life's journey as a pilgrimage and a search and goes on to highlight the nature of the quest. Finding the right kind of analogy of the medieval quest romances, he believes that the final destination of the questing hero is the place of everlasting happiness and eternal, absolute bliss.

As T.S. Eliot says in the last movement of Little Gidding,

We shall never cease from exploration
And the end of our exploring

> Will be to arrive where we started
> And know the place for the first time.
>
> (*Four Quartets*)

Howard Murphet quotes from *The Secret of the Golden Flower*:

> Wandering in Heaven one eats the spirit of energy of the Receptive and the still deeper secret within the secret the land that is nowhere that is the true home.

The place is none other than the Grail castle, the destination of Sir Percival, Sir Galhad and other valiant knights. When the seeker comes finally to the chapel perilous, he has to encounter the grail girl who asks him questions. It is only when he has the gift of grace that he is able to give the right answers and has glimpses of the holy grail. The Grail king is none other than God himself who lives in the inner chambers of the heart of the questor, the inner spirit, the true self. Mr. Murphet significantly says: 'My own Grail castle was my star in the East, Sai Baba.'

Similar has been the experience of many close devotees of Sri Sathya Sai Baba who have bathed in the white radiance of the divine Light and have had glimpses of the Grail, the innermost meaning and purpose of life. When Sai Baba unequivocally declares

> ...the fact that the worship of the Lord in any form, in any name is the worship of Sai or that it is he who grants the boons irrespective of the God to whom you make your prayer, supplication.

what is meant is that the power that operates in and through Sai form is identical to the power to which you pray.

(Quoted by C. Balasingham, *Sai Baba and the Hindu Theory of Evolution*, pp. 54-55)

This is clearly an unmistakable and authentic manifestation of Satchidananda who has a human form, feet and hands and is engaged in purposeful activity of listening to the prayers of the world in pain and misery and is entirely capable of liberating all souls in the universe. That is why God is described as *uttam Purush,* the source of Light, Love and Bliss.

It is the universal omniscience, omnipresence, power, glory and splendour of the highest magnitude that give credence to the belief that Sri Sathya Sai Baba is the manifestation of the divine principle and is the crowned knot of fire and the beacon light by which we know of the glory of God Almighty. As Mr. S.P. Ruhela says:

> Sai Baba has served, inspired and instructed unnumbered thousands of devotees, sceptics, critics and curiosity seekers through the years with profound spiritual powers. One of these is his widely reported capacity to heal the diseases and infirmities of people by blessing them...Another important area of his power is the ability to respond immediately to prayers or cries for help from devotees often hundreds or thousands of miles away by appearing at the site and taking action by materializing gifts of *vibhuti* or other things in their houses by causing message to appear for them, and so on. This divine television and teleprinter has surprised and baffled physical scientists in India and abroad who have seen their laws of Physics fall before Baba's miracles.
>
> (S.P. Ruhela ed., *Sai Baba and His Message,* Intro. x-xi)

And furthermore, he describes the universal charisma of the *Avatar* by testifying to his acceptance as a symbol of divinity by the world at large. He says:

> Devoted Christians have testified that they find in Sai Baba glimpses of their Christ. The Hindus find in him the living images of Shiva, Shakti, Krishna, Rama, or their family deities. The Muslims call him Allah and people of other religions find in him their own conception of God. He is secular, casteless, classless, countryless, religionless, fearless and full of the love of a thousand mothers.
>
> (S.P. Ruhela, *op. cit.,* xi)

Sri Sathya Sai Baba has declared:

> My power is immeasurable. My truth is inexplicable. I am announcing this about me as the need has arisen...Let me tell you that emphatic declarations of the truth of *avatars* were made so clearly and so unmistakably only by Krishna.
>
> (Sathya Sai Baba, *Who is Sai*)

Finally, to write about the principle of divinity emergent in a full Avatar like Sai Baba, is a difficult and precarious business because one cannot enclose the sun in a little room and say with certainty he is this and that. So it would be fair to close this chapter by quoting the words of Howard Murphet:

> If we were asked to list the attributes in our concept of God, the spiritual parent, most of us would name these: compassionate concern for our welfare, the knowledge of what that welfare truly is, the stern strength to make us take the nasty medicine when necessary, the power to help and guide us along the narrow way to our spiritual home, the forgiveness and mercy of the father who welcomes with joy the prodigal, the power to bring essential innovations to the human drama which he himself has created, and a love that is equal towards all his human children. These are the salient qualities in man's mental image of God. And these qualities—all of them—those who have eyes to see have seen in Sai Baba.
>
> (Howard Murphet, *Sai Baba: Man of Miracles,* p. 207)

3

ARDHANARISHWARA

It is a common belief in the minds of many devotees of Sri Sathya Sai Baba that he is a ray from the ultimate Absolute, the Supreme Brahman. But this is a belief that has no basis in the scriptures. On the contrary, the popular accepted notion about *Avatars* is that they are all manifestations of Vishnu or Narayana who is one of the trine Godhead, the others being Brahma, the creator and Shiva, the destroyer. Vishnu is the god who is responsible for the preservation, maintenance and upkeep of the created universe. Whenever virtue is on decline and vice predominates and is on the ascendant owing to the evil actions of the children of the earth, Vishnu or Narayana takes upon himself to restore the balance. For the establishment of the moral order, for sustaining the good and virtuous men and punishing the wicked and vicious ones, in short, for establishing the norms of *sanatan dharma* he incarnates from age to age. Sri Sathya Sai Baba has to say something very significant about the advent of *avatars:*

> Of the *avatars*, some are for a definite limited purpose, like Vamana or Narasimha. They are just manifestations to counter some particular evils. They are not full-fledged, long-lasting, expansive like Rama and Krishna.
>
> (*Sathya Sai Speaks,* 4, p. 154)

For this reason, some *avatars* are born with only the powers requisite for the task at hand. Others, such as Sri Sathya Sai Baba, are endowed with powers beyond the immediate need. The Rama *avatar* manifested some of his powers through his brothers. However, Krishna was a full *avatar,* an incarnation with complete divine powers. Sri Sathya Sai Baba has pointed out the distinction between partial and full *avatars* when he says:

> That is to say, the *avatar* might manifest only such part of the divine glory as was essential for the task which brought the form or it might exceed the limited purpose for which it came and shine in full grandeur. Rama is a good example of the first and Krishna of the second.
>
> (*Sathya Sai Speaks*, 4, p. 132)

Elucidating the reason behind his incarnation in the *kaliyuga* Sri Sathya Sai Baba says:

> The Lord comes as *avatar* when he is anxiously awaited by saints and sages. Sadhus prayed—and I have come.
>
> (*Sathya Sai Speaks*, 4, p. 8)

Howard Murphet records:

> One day, many years ago, I said to Sai Baba, 'Swamiji, the Indian scriptures say that all major *avatars* are descents of Lord Vishnu, but people say that you are an *avatar* of Lord Shiva. How is that?' He smiled and replied, 'It's all one; there is only One.' I knew, by then, that his main teaching was that there is only one God and He goes by many names and appears in many forms. Yet, there are three main facets of the many-faceted one God. The Indian scriptures name these as Brahma, Vishnu and Shiva. So I came to accept the idea that Sai Baba was an *Avatar* of the one God, with emphasis on the Shiva aspect.
>
> (Howard Murphet, *Where the Road Ends*, p. 192)

But there are other evidences that of the recorded annals of Indian cultural and religious myths and legends as well as the more authentic and irrefutable admission of Sri Sathya Sai Baba himself that he is the composite manifestation of both Shiva and his divine consort Shakti, which really means that he is *Ardhanarishwara,* the androgynous God, the combination of the masculine power and executive energy represented by the feminine principle, that is both *Purusha* and *Prakriti.* When the Eternal Absolute incarnates as Rama, Krishna or Sai, there is Maha Lakshmi and Maha Kali as well. The feminine principle is also a cosmic force incarnating as Durga or Kali. It is only rarely that Shiva and Shakti come together and if they do, a terrible beauty is born. There exists a story in the annals of Aryan culture. Sage Bhardwaj spent a lifetime in the quest of knowledge and complete and thorough mastery over the sacred Vedas. But even after a life span of one hundred years, devoted and consecrated to that thirst for Vedic knowledge, he realized that he was merely standing at the shore of the ocean only gathering pebbles and the pearls still lay hidden in the depth of the ocean. Feeling sad and disconsolate and faint on account of withering old age, he approached Indra, the king of Gods, and prayed to him for lengthening his life further. The boon of another hundred years was granted to him and he resumed his quest with additional vigour. Time passed and the fresh lease of hundred years of life came to an end. But sage Bhardwaj felt that the ocean of knowledge lay still before him and he was thirsty and insatiated as ever. The knowledge was limitless and infinite and life too short. Although he was granted three centuries of existence, at the end of the period, he stayed on the fringe of Vedic knowledge. He approached Indra again and renewed his plaint. This time Indra praised him for his great unquenchable thirst for knowledge and his consistency, and advised him to organize a *yagna* and invite the primeval divine mother Parvati to preside over the *yagna*. Indra assured him that this would crown his effort and enable him to garner the true and full knowledge of the sacred lore. Sage Bhardwaj actually did organize a full-fledged *yagna* and travelled to the snow-capped Mount Kailash, the abode of Lord Shiva and divine mother, Shakti. Since the divine couple were engaged in their cosmic dance, Sage Bhardwaj waited for full eight days in intense and freezing cold of the region. Mother Shakti appeared before him and indicated through her gesture that she would attend his *yagna;* but unfortunately, Bhardwaj failed to understand her positive sign. Utterly exhausted and disconsolate, the sage turned around to go back. No sooner than he took a few steps on the frozen terrain he fell down on the icy ground and his left limbs were paralyzed. Lord Shiva and Parvati both saw him fall. Shankar, the compassionate Lord, moved towards the sage and raised him. He sprinkled few drops of water on the body of the sage from his *kamandulu* and spoke to him in soft and sweet words:

> 'Bhardwaj, Parvati and I will grace your *yagna* with our presence and your desire to gain Vedic knowledge will be crowned with success.'

And he further conferred another important boon by saying that he would incarnate in *kaliyuga* thrice in order to bless his *gotra* and lineage. Lord Shiva went on to say: 'In my second manifestation in *kaliyuga* when I would be known as Sathya Sai and would live in that body along with Shakti then this Shakti would remain immobile and motionless and would suffer a similar inertia, pain and paralysis as you have suffered here under the frozen cold.' Thus, the boon vouchsafed to sage Bhardwaj has come to fructify in the *kaliyuga*. First, Lord Shiva manifested himself as Sai Baba of Shirdi in Maharashtra State, and later at Puttaparthi in Andhra Pradesh as Sathya Sai Baba, the composite androgynous God, *ardhanarishwara,* the masculine and feminine aspect of Shiva and Shakti rolled into one. Sri Sathya Sai Baba has prophesied that the triple Sai incarnation would take place at Mandya district in Karnataka after he attains *maha samadhi* at the age of ninety-six years.

The point to note here is that all this is not mere fancy or fairy tale. If we cast a glance at the advent of Sai Baba of Shirdi, the circumstances of his birth, his arrival at the Shirdi village and making it his playground for his *leela* and his splendour and majesty, the truth of the matter is revealed. Besides, we have the account given by Sai Baba himself:

> I propose to reveal what has not been known to anyone hitherto. In the former Nizam's dominions there was a remote village called Pathri. In that village there was a couple named Ganga Bhavadiya and Devagiriamma. They are grieving over lack of children. In answer to their prayer, a son was born on September 28th, 1858. That child was Sai Baba...On Vijayadashmi day in 1918, he gave up the body.

(Sathya Sai Baba, quoted by V.K. Gokak, *Sai Baba: Man and Avatar*, p. 64)

In a detailed and longish account, Sri Sathya Sai Baba says how Parmeshwar and Parvati appeared before Devagiriamma and told him that they were pleased with her devotion and that Lord

Shiva would take birth as her third child. The divine blessing fructified and the child was born on the road while the couple were on way to the forest, renouncing the world and in search of Parmeshwar and Parvati. The abandoned child was picked up by a Sufi *fakir* who brought him up. After the passing away of the *fakir*, his wife took care of the child. The child behaved in a strange manner. He went to the Hindu temples and proclaimed that he was Allah and visited mosques, shouting that Rama was God. Upset by the troublesome behaviour, the widow of the *fakir* placed him in the *ashram* of Venkusa. He left the *ashram* and reached Shirdi in 1858, and stayed there for two months. He wandered from place to place until he reached Shirdi again with marriage party of Chandu Patel's brother's son. He remained there for sixty years. The divinity of Shirdi Sai Baba was revealed. Once while playing with marble with a neighbour boy, he swallowed the marble which was a lingam. The mother of the boy was greatly incensed and rushed to the place, demanding the sacred Lingam. As Babu, as Shirdi Baba was called, opened his mouth, the bewildered woman was awestruck as she saw creations and universes rolling one after the other. She knelt down before the child and knew that she was face to face with Lord Shiva himself. When asked by his devotees, Sai Baba predicted that he would come again as a boy of fourteen in the south, and it so happened that Sri Sathya Sai Baba was born on November 23, 1926 at Puttaparthi in Andhra Pradesh, and he declared at the age of fourteen in 1940 that he was Sai Baba.

Furthermore, Sri Sathya Sai Baba has also revealed the events that took place in the *Sathyayuga* that testifies to the truth of Lord Shiva's boon conferred on sage Bhardwaj. In the words of Sri Sathya Sai Baba:

> For those who have no refuge, God is the refuge. That is exactly the reason why I had to take on the disease that one helpless devotee was otherwise to get. He would have had to suffer this dire illness as well as four heart attacks which accompanied it, and he would not have survived. So according to my *dharma* of *bhaktha samrakshana,* I had to rescue him.
>
> There is another reason, too, why the eight-day period had

to be observed—something I have not disclosed so far, something which I have been keeping within myself for the last thirty-seven years. The time has come to announce it.

Thousands of years ago, the great sage Bhardwaj, wishing to master all the Vedas, was advised by Indra to perform a *yagna*. Eager to have Shakti, the consort of Shiva, to preside over it and receive her blessings Bhardwaj left for Kailash, the abode of Shiva and Shakti to convey the invitation. Finding them coupled in the cosmic dance, Bhardwaj waited for eight days—apparently ignored by them. Although he had failed to comprehend the welcoming smile cast at him by Shakti. Unhappy and disappointed, Bhardwaj decided to return home. But as he began to descend he fell in a stroke, his left side paralysed as a result of cold and fatigue. Shiva approached and cured him completely by sprinkling on him water from the *kamandulu*. Consoled by Shiva, Bhardwaj was granted boons both by Shiva and Shakti, who also were pleased to attend the *yagna*. Shiva promised the rishi that they would both take human form and be born there in Bhardwaj lineage or *gotra*: Shiva alone at Shirdi, as Sai Baba; Shiva and Shakti together at Puttaparthi as Sathya Sai Baba; then Shakti alone as Prema Sai. Further in expiation of an illness that Bhardwaj had suffered at Kailash, Shiva made another promise. This Shakti will suffer a stroke for eight days when we both take birth as Sathya Sai and on the eighth day I will relieve her from all signs of the disease by sprinkling water just as I did at Kailash to cure your illness. The assurance given in the *Tretha yuga* had to be honoured. The splendour of this *avatar* will go on increasing day by day.

(Sathya Sai Baba, Quoted by Samuel Sandweiss, *Sai Baba: The Holy Man and the Psychiatrist*, pp. 99-100)

No wonder that this emphatic and timely declaration by Sri Sathya Sai Baba that he was truly the embodiment of Shiva and Shakti. Baba says:

Let me tell you. Nothing can impede or halt the work of the *Avatar*. When I was upstairs some people foolishly went about saying 'It is all over with Sai Baba' and they turned

> back many who were coming to Puttaparthi. Some said I was in *samadhi* (communion with God) as if I was a *sadhaka* (Aspirant). Some feared I was a victim of black magic as if anything can affect me...The splendour of this *Avatar* will go on increasing day by day. Formerly, when the Govardhangiri was raised aloft by the little boy Krishna, the Gopis and Gopals (milkmaids and cowherds) realized that Krishna was the Lord. Now not one Govardhangiri but a whole range will be lifted—you will see! Have patience, have faith.
>
> (Sathya Sai Baba, Quoted by Samuel Sandweiss, *Sai Baba: The Holy Man and the Psychiatrist*, p. 101)

When the eternal Absolute and his executive force, Shakti, choose to take human birth, nothing is beyond realization. And as the poet has said, world's great age begins anew and the golden years return. The concept of *Ardhanarishwara* is ingrained in the imagination of the Indian mind. The power and majesty of the Shiva Shakti form acquires the Nth dimension and nothing remains unattainable. As Baba himself states:

> This is a human form in which every divine entity, every divine principle, that is to say, all names and forms ascribed by Man to God are manifest. Do not allow doubt to distract you; if you instal in the altar of your heart steady faith in my reality as *Sarvadevataswarupam* you can soon have a vision of my reality...Let me draw your attention to another fact. On previous occasions, when God incarnated on earth the bliss of recognizing him was vouchsafed only after the physical Embodiment had left the world in spite of plenty of patent evidence of His grace. The loyalty and devotion they commanded but in this age of materialism, what is it that brings to it the adoration of millions from all over the world? The reason is, it is Supra-world Divinity in human form.
>
> (Sathya Sai Baba, 'My Reality', *Garland of 108 Precious Gems*, ed. N. Kasturi, Intro., ii)

Among the one hundred and eight names attributed to Sri Sathya Sai Baba, the most important one is that of Shiva, Sankar or Maheshwar, one of the Hindu Trinity: Brahma the creator, Vishnu the preserver and Mahesh the destroyer.

Shankar is the doer; it is he who confers happiness and prosperity. Sai Baba of Shirdi often used to bless his devotees by saying that in the abode of my devotees there will be no dearth of food and clothing; I will not allow my devotees to come to harm. As a matter of fact, Baba is the universal provider who, like Krishna, is responsible for providing *yogakshema* to all his devotees, the mother who is more loving than all the mothers of the world. To see him is to get oneself rid of sin. To touch his feet is to unburden oneself of the load of *karma*. Baba floods us with happiness. He has the attribute of Shiva, for example, application of *vibhuti* or ash on the body. His grace is easy to earn. He has given visions of himself as Shiva. Many devotees have seen him as Shiva. Sai Baba combines in himself the power of Shiva and Shakti both. He is Shiva-Shakti born together even as they are at Kailash and he grants Shivam, bliss, happiness and shakti, vigour, intelligence. He instils faith in the *Atma* within. Further, as Mr. N. Kasturi says:

> Om Sri Sarva Shakti Moortaye Namah. Moorti means image, idol, symbol, embodiment. Baba is the Moorti of all Shakti (Sarvashakti). He is Mahashakti come as Mayashakti. The innovator of the will, the deed and the thought is He and none else. He is the manifestation of all Godhead which are subsumed in the Sathya Sai form and name. For Baba has granted vision of himself as Shiva-Shakti, as Shakti, as Shiva at Kothanghatta temple and at Hampi Virupaksha temple, as Krishna, as Rama, as Ganesha and as Panduranga.
>
> (N. Kasturi ed., *Garland of 108 Precious Gems*, p. 20)

Further Professor Kasturi says:

> Om Sri Maheshwar *Swaroopaynamah*. Maheshwara is another name of Lord Shiva meaning auspiciousness or profusion of favours. The most meaningful symbol of Shiva is the oval-shaped figure called *Lingam*...Baba creates these symbols of Shiva in himself, on Shivaratri. Shiva is also the third aspect of Divinity, the *Layakaraka*, the merciful God who merges all in the universal, reduces all to the ultimate ash. Maheshwara

> also means the supreme God...Baba is undoubtedly Maheshwara Swaroop.
>
> (N. Kasturi, *op. cit.*, p. 24)

There is a very interesting incident that took place on the roadside three days after Baba's birthday on the 26th November 1958. A devotee from Bangalore left Prasanthi Nilayam by car, taking leave of Baba. This is how Mr. Kasturi describes the incident:

> On the way, his two year old daughter was attacked by fits which became so serious that the child was asphyxiated and collapsed. Baba knew this and presented himself before them as a villager with two other villagers whom he created. He wanted the child to be given to him and the two comrades supported his demand, 'Give him, he will cure it; he has cured thousands,' they implored. The villager (Baba) told them, 'I was busy for the last three days; just now laid myself for rest that a child was seriously ill on the road. So, I ran up.' He placed the child on his lap and it was cured. He gave it back to the happy parents. They offered him a rupee and when it was refused they gave him a fruit—from the many that he himself had given them at the Nilayam while leaving...
>
> They asked him his name. He said Jodi Adiapalli Somappa. When asked at the Nilayam why he chose that name of all others, Baba said, 'I am Somappa Soma appa (Shiva) Sa Uma—Shiva Shakti—twin—Prakriti and Purusha.' He reveals his truth as Shiva-Shakti.
>
> Thus Jodi Adiapalli Somappaya is Baba's most appropriate epithet, selected by himself, for that profound miracle of grace.
>
> (N. Kasturi, *Garland of 108 Precious Gems*, p. 27)

Another name for Sathya Sai Baba relates to the great sage Bhardwaja. Baba announced that he belonged to Bhardwaja *Gotra* or lineage and that he was Sai Baba. This dramatic announcement was made by him at the age of fourteen. And later, in the year 1963 he threw off the paralysis of a devotee which he had taken over and announced to the anxious assembled audience on the Gurupoornima day that he was Shiva-Shakti in human form. Mr. Kasturi says:

> In response to a boon granted to Bhardwaja rishi by Shiva in the past that he would take human form in his Gotra as Sai Baba of Shirdi and as Sathya Sai Baba, He will be born in the same gotra as Prema Sai Baba in the future... Bhardwaja's ashram was at Prayag; he is mentioned in the *Ramayana* as a sage with amazing spiritual powers, won by *thapas.* Baba declared that he was not Sathyanarayan Raju as people knew him till then, that was only a make-belief, worn by him until the world could grasp the news of his Divinity. Even his claim to the Gotra of Bhardwaja is a make-belief, for how can the Divine be bound by lineage and kin?
>
> (N. Kasturi, *op. cit.,* p. 28)

It follows from this that Sai Baba is the incarnation of the one supreme God, the manifestation of the Divine principle as *Aadi Shakti* and *Aadi Purusha.* Mr. Kasturi discusses the implication of all this when he says:

> Baba is the *Avatar* of the age, come to restore *Dharma* and save man from downfall. He is the *sanatana sarathi,* the eternal charioteer. One of his acts as charioteer was at Kurukshetra when he instructed Arjuna in the science of Liberation...Baba is *sanatana sarathi,* the primeval *Purusha*...This means he was and is in the past and the present. *Aadi* means the 'very first'. The Lord is the very first person, the digit that gives value to the zeros that he granted a vision of himself as Padmanabh to Swami Purushotamananda at Vashishta Guha near the Ganga, near Rishikesh.
>
> (N. Kasturi, *op. cit.,* pp. 57-58)

So we can conclude that Sri Sathya Sai Baba is the *avatar* of the Supreme Brahman, the Eternal Absolute in human form. But in another sense, he is the living configuration of the masculine and feminine aspect of the one God. In the words of N. Kasturi:

> Many devotees experience Bhagwan Sri Sathya Sai Baba as their mother. So deep is his love and his consideration for

the comfort and progress of his children! Baba has himself declared that he is Shiva-Shakti. He often describes Prasanthi Nilayam to women devotees as 'your own mother's house'. Baba is Aadi Shakti; the energy aspect of the *Aadi purush.* This energy is believed to be feminine and is worshipped as such during *Navratri,* the festival of the mother, of Aadi Shakti (prime energy). Baba evinces that he himself is Saraswati, Durga and Lakshmi. He has the overpowering love of the Supreme Mother.

(*Garland of 108 Precious Gems,* p. 58)

No one with equal or more shakti has appeared on earth, since Lord Krishna except the Sai Shakti...Sai Baba at Shirdi declared he was Basudeva. 'I am Mahalaxmi, I am Vinoba of Pandari, I am Ganpati, I am Dattatreya, I am Krishna. All this universe is me. I am formless and everywhere; all that is seen is my form...' Sathya Sai Baba, the same Baba who has come again, is as universal and as omnipotent as the Sai who declared, 'I am the universal Absolute that is both immanent and transcendent, I am Viswa-Virat-Swarup, I am Sarva-devata-Swarup...' 'When someone asks you where God is, do not dodge the question giving a reply in which you have no faith, namely, 'He is everywhere'. Direct him to Puttaparthi', He has declared.

(*Garland of 108 Precious Gems,* p. 59)

Professor N. Kasturi says further about Sai Baba:

Baba was sought as a son by his mother Easwaramba through a series of Sathyanarayan *vrathas* (worship): so he was named Sathyanarayan and called Sathya until his fourteenth year, when he judged the time had come to announce that he was no other than Sai Baba (The real and the genuine Sai Baba). Millions know him as Sai Baba or Sathya Sai Baba. Sai means Lord, master. It also means Sa: Sarveshwara, sovereign; Ayi means mother; Baba means father; Sai means glory in all respect.

(*Garland of 108 Precious Gems,* p. 11)

It has become common knowledge now that Sri Sathya Sai

Baba is the Avatar of the age comparable in power and splendour to Krishna and Christ, and is worshipped by millions all over the world. Enlightened spiritual seekers, eminent intellectuals, scientists and devotees ranging from the highest to the lowest ranks of society pay their obeisance at the lotus feet of Baba and regard him with deepest reverence, ardour and sense of self-surrender. N. Kasturi, the eminent biographer of Baba, has absolutely no doubt about the true identity of Baba and says that Swami has not assumed the form of an ordinary human being. 'He is the three-role presentation of cosmic consciousness: Supreme Brahman, Iswara, the creator and Avatar, the Incarnation.' Professor Kasturi, having spent thirty years in all waking consciousness with Sai Baba, affirms the truth of Swami's concrete, tangible presence as God in human form. Sai Baba has himself said that the Sai form is the form of all the various names that man uses for the adoration of the Divine and that no distinction should be made between the names of Rama, Krishna, Iswara and Sai. Since our concern here in this chapter is with the Hindu concept of Ardhanarishwara, that is the combined manifestation of Shiva and Shakti, *purusha* and *prakriti* we take it that both the male and female adjuncts of the one God are operative in the Sai form according to the grand *Avataric* design known only to God Almighty. The manifestation of triple Sai avatar seems imminent. Sri Sathya Sai Baba has himself explained the logic of the successive advents in Kaliyuga to Mr. R.K. Karanjia, the editor of *Blitz* magazine. This is truly revealing and has to be quoted in full:

> Q. Why had this task to be divided in three separate incarnations of the Shirdi, Sathya and Prema Babas?
>
> Baba: They are not separate. I have already mentioned the complete oneness of the three in the final objective of the mission. I will give you an example. Take a kilo of *gur* (a sweet substance). The whole of it tastes sweet. Now break it in small pieces. Each of it tastes sweet. Finally break them further into small grains. You find the same sweetness in them. So the difference is one of quantity and not quality. It is the same with *Avatars*. Their tasks and powers requisite

> to them differ according to the time, the situation and the environment. But they belong to and derive from the same *dharma swarup* or divine body.
>
> Let us take the example of fruit. It begins with the seed which grows into the tree and from it comes the fruit. Work can be compared to the seed, worship to the tree, and wisdom to the fruit...The previous *Avatar*, Shirdi Baba laid the base for secular integration and gave mankind the message of duty is work. The mission of the present *Avatar* is to make everybody realize that the same God or divinity resides in everyone. People should respect, love and help each other irrespective of colour or creed. Thus all work can become a way of worship. Finally, Prema Sai, the third *Avatar* will promote the evangel news that not only does God reside in everybody, but everybody is God. That will be the final wisdom which will enable every man and woman to go to God. The three *Avatars* carry the triple message of Work, Worship and Wisdom.
>
> (Quoted by Samuel Sandweiss, *Spirit and the Mind*, pp. 236-37)

However, the embodiment of Shiva and Shakti together in the figure of Sathya Sai Baba adds a new and additional dimension to the majesty, glory and grandeur of this manifestation. When before the *Gurupoornima* day in 1963, he had suffered a stroke and a series of four major heart attacks and the doctors diagnosed tubercular meningitis, Baba refused to take medicines and injections, saying that he would be alright in four days' time. And actually on the evening of Gurupoornima, Baba descended the circular stairs down to the prayer hall. He sat on the chair before five thousand, silent and sorrowful people. Then he gestured for water, drank some, and sprinkled some drops on the paralysed left hand and stroked the stiff left leg and hand. And then the miracle of all miracles happened. Swami become immediately normal, cured of all his infirmity, stood up before the audience and delivered his address in clear, and resonant voice and continued for an hour. The devotees danced with joy.

As prophesied by Lord Shiva in *Treta yuga* to sage Bhardwaja Sathya Sai Baba who was born as Shiva-Shakti in one enacted the miracle of healing his paralysed left limb (Shakti) by his right hand (Shiva).

As Baba declared in that Gurupoornima address, his divinity had to be announced by the manifestation of the grand miracle, his taking over the disease of a forlorn devotee was just incidental.

Finally if we cast a glance at the circumstances and situations before the birth of Baba on November 23, 1926, we come to know that many strange, inexplicable, divine phenomena were witnessed. One such strange phenomenon was that the musical instruments placed in the Raju household, *tambura, mridang* etc. started playing by themself transmitting unearthly music, the significance of which was difficult to grasp. Venkappa Raju, the father, was deeply concerned about the event and was, more or less, apprehensive. So he visited as many as six nearby villages and contacted wise and sacred men about it. One Shastri, in whom Venkappa Raju had full faith, dispelled his fear and apprehension by saying that the mysterious music was all for the good, an auspicious sign, a harbinger of great things to come. Venkappa Raju testified to the fact that supranatural music was so captivating and bewitching that he could not find words to describe its beauty. Then Shastri told him that a divine power was to be born and that the gods were heralding his birth by playing on the musical instruments to welcome it. On the 23rd November in the early morning six minutes past five A.M., the advent of the Lord took place. It was the month of Kartik and Lakshamma, the mistress of the house and wife of Kodamma Raju, was attending the worship of God Satyanarayan at the house of a neighbour. She was informed; but she came only after the Pooja was over. She offered the *prasad* to Eswaramma and soon afterward she delivered the child. The child was put by the grandmother on a bed. Seeing the movement, akin to the rise and fall of the bed, the family members discovered that a cobra was lying under the bed. This was an entirely strange and inexplicable event. Although the serpents frequented the village homes, it was unbelievable that a serpent would enter the bed-room and station itself under a freshly prepared bed. Surely, that serpent must have been the Adishesh on which Lord Vishnu was resting. Biographers and commentators find in this extraordinary and unbelievable occurrence the evidence of the first great miracle soon after the birth of the divine child. Another strange event that surprised Eswaramma was the presence of aura of bright light round the face of the child. Sacred ash or *vibhuti* came out of the body of the divine child establishing his kinship and identity with Shiva, the supreme God. It all proved beyond doubt that the child was no other than Lord Shiva himself, the cosmic visitor from the ultimate beyond to shed his lustre and glory on earth and its inhabitants. Sathyanarayan Raju was growing like waxing moon in the sky and became the universal favourite of the village. His grandfather Kodamma Raju was very fond of him. It seemed to him that his prayer to Venka Avadoot had been answered. When Sathyanarayan started going to the school at Bukkapatnam, he was admired by his playmates. They called him Guru and *Brahmagyani*. The account of Sathyanarayan Raju's earlier life is recorded in its full detail and texture by Professor N. Kasturi in *Sathyam, Sivam, Sundaram*, the most authentic biography of Sai Baba. One may say without hesitation that the early phase of Sai Baba's life and career announces the presence of a power that was destined to move the world and ensure the advent of a millennium. Sathyanarayan Raju endeared himself to all alike and established his credentials as a gentle and pleasing personality with extraordinary charisma, intelligence and great interest in singing, dancing, feeding the poor and composing religious songs and staging plays on religious and moral themes. He would often surprise his friends and classmates by materializing objects like sweets, toffies, *vibhuti*, lemon drops, etc. He also joined a circus party to sing and dance. In one such dance, he even surpassed a famous dancer of the theatre. No wonder, he was Shiva, the cosmic dancer. On May 23, 1940, he disclosed to his father and other members of the family 'I am Sai Baba. I belong to the Apastamba sutra, the school of sage Apastamba and am of the spiritual lineage of sage Bhardwaja. I am Sai Baba of Shirdi. I have come to ward off your troubles; keep your houses clean and pure.'

It was later on October 20, 1940, while he was staying with his elder brother Seshama Raju at Urvakonda and studying in class VIII at the high school there, that he cast aside his books and standing at the doorstep of his brother's house, he declared: 'I am no longer your Sathya. I am Sai.' His sister-in-law came out of the kitchen and as she looked at the face of Sathyanarayan Raju, she was almost blinded by the bright aura hovering around the face and she shrieked. Baba addressed her: 'I am going. I don't belong to you. Illusion has gone. My devotees are calling me. I have my work. I cannot stay any longer.' As every step in the career of an *Avatar* is predetermined, the time had come for Baba to reveal his true identity. Thus, the assurance given by Sai Baba of Shirdi to his close disciples Abdul Baba, Kaka Dixit and others, that he would come again in the South as a boy of fourteen had come true. Baba was just fourteen years of age at that time. His parents came from Puttaparthi and made all efforts to persuade him to return home. All that they could get from him was the assurance that he would return on the condition that his work should not be hampered and he would live away from the ancestral home. Thus, he moved to the house of Subamma, who, like Yashoda, proved to be his foster mother who looked after him and his devotees who thronged the village in increasing numbers. On the 23rd birthday of Baba, the devotees constructed the spacious *Ashram* with a prayer hall about a mile away from Puttaparthi village and Baba blessed it. It was named Prashanthi Nilayam, the abode of peace, which now has become a place of pilgrimage for millions from all the nooks and corners of the world. Like Lourdes in Spain, it has become a power substation, the residence of God on earth. Baba has carried on his mission of *Dharma sthapana* and *Bhakta samrakshana* ever since. He operates on two levels. As human being made of flesh and blood, he meets an increasing number of people from all parts of the world and works ceaselessly for their welfare and moral uplift. It is in this sense that his life is his message. More than this, he operates on the level of a mysterious divine Spirit, as an omnipotent and omnipresent God and as dispenser of Divine justice to all his children. He is the Eternal Absolute, a Ray from the primeval Fire, the single flame that is God, the *Ardhanarishwara* who unites in himself the Divine Principle as Idea and executive energy, the masculine and feminine aspect of creation.

It is not possible for human intelligence to grasp the full implication of *Ardhanarishwara*. In the first incarnation we have seen that it was Lord Shiva himself who walked the earth; in the second, the divine couple Iswara and Parvati both took human form as Sathya Sai Baba. And Prema Sai is still to come, presumably in the first quarter of the next century and he will be the embodiment of Shakti. And then, the triple Sai Incarnation will come full circle and the divine mission for which the Lord is pleased to take human form would inevitably be crowned with success.

At the end of this chapter, it may be rewarding to echo the view of the poet, V.K. Gokak, about the Shiva-Shakti aspect of Sri Sathya Sai Baba. It is the considered opinion of the present author that obtuse and difficult metaphysical problems can be viewed by one through the perspective of poetry. It is verily the poet who gets at the centre of the reality that *is*. Again it is the poet who gives a concrete, tangible expression to what may seem to the average men tenuous, vague and dissolving abstractions. V.K. Gokak in his beautiful poem, *Darshan,* sums up the *ardhanarishwara* aspect of Sri Sathya Sai Baba in the following verses:

Have you seen Baba
Who sets cities aflame with longing
And drenches them with the delight of existence?
You've missed the very meaning of your life
If you haven't seen him and been spoken to by him.

....

He defies the laws of physics and chemistry
That he might assert the higher laws of spirit
A lingam materialises
That a million souls may be born.

Matter and spirit are Siamese twins
That have an identical body but a different face
Only the androgynous God—
Ardhanarishwara—
Purusha and Shakti in one—
Can solve the riddle of their birth and growth.

('Darshan', *Sai Baba: Man and Avatar,* pp. 82-83)

4

SAI BABA AND JESUS OF NAZARETH

Sai Baba's closest parallel is Jesus of Nazareth, the son of God. Jesus, the Christ, is believed to be the only incarnation of the Holy Spirit, in human form who came to bring about the spiritual regeneration of mankind through the gospel of love, faith, charity and hope. He was subjected to endless suffering, pain and torture at the hands of the Philistines, and finally was put on the cross and embraced death so that mankind may live and attain the kingdom of heaven. Jesus Christ performed countless number of miracles, even the raising of the dead so that God may be glorified. The raising of Lazarus is indeed a classic example of his God-like power. Being the son of God, he could perform any miracle, such as multiplying the quantity of food and curing the sick and the diseased. In the pages of the Holy Bible, we read the numerous instances of the miraculous deeds of Christ, most of these being performed to glorify God and instil faith in the minds of the people. When he resurrected Lazarus four days after his corpse was decomposing in the tomb, he did so mainly because he wanted to show to the sisters of Lazarus and his friends the supreme glory of the Divine. Another reason for this interference with the laws of nature lay in his deep love and great compassion for Martha and Mary, the devoted sisters of Lazarus. Then there is the question of faith and total surrender to Almighty God. The resurrection of Lazarus demonstrates very clearly the fact that faith is a vital factor. Both Martha and Mary had expressed the view that had Jesus been there, their brother would not have died. So Jesus, when he came to know about the death of Lazarus, went to the place where the body had been buried in the tomb and he called out: 'Lazarus, come out.' And the miracle took place instantly. Lazarus came out of the grave. The fact remains that faith and God's power may interfere with the cosmic laws and even halt or prevent death from coming and invoke God's mercy to grant a fresh lease of life to a person. Faith, however, does not envisage that there will be no more deaths or that death will have no dominion. Though Lazarus was called back from the tomb, some years later he died. Similar is the case with the aged American, Walter Cowan, whom Sai Baba brought back to life. He also died a few years later. The temporary respite from death enables the person to apprehend the plans of the divine and gain some measure of spiritual illumination. However, according to Hindu religious thought, cessation of consciousness is a *karmic* event and falls in the pattern of the cycle of birth, death, rebirth. Sai Baba has said both in his previous and present incarnations that to cure a certain person, to save from death or to remove some inborn physical blemish would be to interfere unduly with a person's *karma*. And in such cases, it is better to leave the person concerned to bear the consequences of his *karma*. Howard Murphet has rightly said:

> As mankind is today we cannot expect Sai Baba or any other God-powered man to dissolve the whole cloud of Man's *karmic* sins, curing all diseases, making all the cripples walk, cleansing all the lepers, opening the eyes of millions of blind that exist in India alone. The most he can do is to lift a little of the *karma* here and there and point the way.
>
> (*Sai Baba: Man of Miracles*, p. 137)

And speaking about the reality and significance of the miraculous, he further says:

> A God-man, a living worker of miracles, will be able through global communications to travel the world and to make his message known to all the people during his lifetime...Of old this could not happen and tiding of such amazing events reached the mass of mankind either through verbal reports or by accounts written long after the events took place. Now the sceptic, the doubting Thomas who cannot believe in the lesser or greater miracles can prove their reality to himself.

> If keen enough, he can visit Prasanthi Nilayam to witness them; otherwise he can wait until Sai Baba comes to his part of the world. The miracles of Krishna and Christ must be taken on trust or faith; those of Sai Baba you can see for yourself.
>
> (*Sai Baba: Man of Miracles*, p. 189)

Returning to the momentous and magnificent miracle, resurrection of the dead, one finds some concrete and easily verifiable incidents when Sai Baba, like Jesus Christ, has blessed his close devotees with special grace and has granted them a fresh lease of life. It seems, this miracle of resurrection has to do with the transfiguring power of love and works like the coming together of the negative and positive currents of electricity. Baba has emphasised this aspect time and again. In his interview with R.K. Karanjia, he says:

> Q. You are believed to have performed miraculous cures to the extent of resurrecting the dead. There are cases where you reportedly have saved people from drowning and other accidents in distant places. Medical experts have attested to remote-controlled surgical operations performed by you. How do you manage this?
>
> Baba: By my own *sankalpa*—that is divine will and power. As an *Avatar*, this power is intrinsic, inherent, total and natural to my will and decision. I need no *mantras* (mystical formula), no *sadhana* (spiritual practice) and no *yantra* (mechanism) to perform the so-called miracles which are natural to my state. My powers are simply the expression or assertion of the reality of Godliness which merges me with everything everywhere, at all times and places. The miracles belong to the boundless power of God. Now coming to the main points of your question, this healing phenomenon has a dual aspect. I can cure, save even resurrect people provided they are in a spiritually receptive condition. It is like the positive and negative currents of electricity. My capacity to heal can be compared to the positive current. Your devotion to me is the negative current. Once the two come together,

the devotion provides what is called the miracle of healing.

(Quoted by Samuel Sandweiss, *Spirit and the Mind*, p. 242)

In the days of Christ, no one asked him the rationale of his amazing and unique miracles of healing. However, if asked, he too would have given a similar explanation because, in the ultimate analysis, it is faith and love that lie at the root of all miracles. Truly, miracles are wrought by faith and love. In the case of the official's daughter, when Jesus saw her sleeping, he said that she was sleeping; her sleep was not unto death. And he called her to wake up. And again, in the case of Lazarus, he said the same thing and asked Lazarus to come out of the tomb. He further said that he revived or resurrected him so that God, the Father, might be glorified by this act. On the other hand, Sai Baba of Shirdi always maintained that Allah was the universal master, the doer of all deeds and thinker of all thoughts, and that he was the servant of that Eternal Absolute. All he could do to remove the suffering of his devotees who had surrendered to him and left everything to him, was to use his influence with Almighty Supreme God. And many a miraculous cure took place. Jesus Christ also used to directly address God, the Father: 'I know you listen to me and fulfil all my wishes and requests.' And it was on the basis of such direct intervention that Lazarus came out of the tomb. The point to note here is that the doer and the granter of the boons is none other than the Supreme transcendental power. But an *Avatar* has the power to operate on behalf of the one God whose attributes have been transferred to him as a substation from the vast power grid.

The event of the resurrection of two ardent and sincere devotees, Radhakrishna and Walter Cowan, is too well known to be described in detail. In Howard Murphet's *Sai Baba: Man of Miracles* and Samuel Sandweiss's *Sai Baba: The Holy Man and the Psychiatrist,* we find a full and adequate account of the resurrection story. Here it may be enough to describe the ultimate emotional reaction of Elsie Cowan the wife of Walter Cowan and that of Radhakrishna himself.

Mr. V. Radhakrishna of Kuppam, Andhra Pradesh, paid a visit to Puttaparthi along with his wife, daughter Vijaya and K.S

Hemchand, his son-in-law. They were staying in a room at the *ashram.* One evening, he was suddenly taken ill and soon went into a coma. His wife immediately rushed to Swami and informed him about the condition of her husband. Swami came to the room where the patient was lying on the bed. Swami did nothing and he returned saying: 'Don't worry, everything will be all right.' But the condition of the patient worsened through the next and subsequent two days. He lay unconscious with no signs of life, cold and lifeless. In sheer desperation and unable to withstand the pressure of the *Ashramites* for taking out the body that was beginning to stink, for the last rites, Mrs. Radhakrishna once again went to Swami's apartment and told him all. Swami laughed and assured her that she should have no fear and he promised to visit her room to see the patient. Mrs. Radhakrishna, Vijaya and Hemchand waited, desolate, tense and apprehensive, hoping for some unexpected miracle. Swami eventually came to the room and entered the patient's room and the others stayed out. Swami was alone in the room with the dead patient. He called others to the room after some time and as the close kins entered the room, they were amazed and wonder-struck to see Radhakrishna sitting on the bed, as though he had woken up after a deep slumber. Swami turned to the wife and said, 'I have given your husband back to you.' When questioned by Mr. Howard Murphet, Mr. Radhakrishna narrated his experience in the following words, 'When I became conscious again, I thought at first that it was the same day. Later they told me it had been three days I was unconscious, that I was dead and actually started to stink. But Swami can do anything he wishes. He is God.'

(*Sai Baba: Man of Miracles,* p. 133)

Mr. Radhakrishna is the fortunate one who has assumed the role of a modern Lazarus in order to remind a sceptical and faithless age of the power and potency of God Almighty. His story has been checked and verified and found to be correct and authentic. Mr. Howard Murphet has himself taken pains to get the irrefutable evidence from Vijaya, the daughter of Radhakrishna.

The resurrection story of Walter Cowan is far more exciting

and unique for it illustrates what Divine love can do. It is an instance of the transfiguring and transcendent power of love and the deathless ardour of a devotee. This time the Lazarus in question is an American devotee, Walter Cowan of California who had lived a noble life of service and dedication to the highest human values, work and worship. The facts of the case are as follows:

Walter and his wife Elsie Cowan arrived in Madras on December 23, 1971. On the morning of the 25th of December, word went round that an elderly American had passed away on account of a fatal heart attack. On hearing the news, John Hislop, an American devotee from Mexico, rushed to the hotel and met Elsie Cowan who confirmed the news. She narrated how Walter had suffered the attack and breathed his last in the arms of Elsie Cowan who had prayed to Swami during those moments of crisis and had got herself reconciled to the reality of death and felt that God's will will be done. However, with the help of Mrs. Roshan Lal, a devotee of Baba, she arranged to take Walter to the hospital where the attending physician pronounced him to be dead. In the meantime Elsie Cowan rushed to the place where Baba was attending a function. After some time when she went again to the hospital, she found to her dismay and pleasant wonder that Walter Cowan was very much alive. The matter was brought to the notice of the attending physician who had pronounced Walter to be dead and had sent the dead body to a room with his ears stuffed and a sheet over the body as he was absolutely certain that the patient was dead. Fortunately, the whole matter was investigated by Justice Damodar Rao and all evidence proved that Walter Cowan who was dead had come back to life. During the period between his death and reported resurrection, it came to everybody's knowledge that Sai Baba had himself visited the hospital in response to the prayer of Elsie Cowan. It is also on record that at the hospital during the course of subsequent days, Walter's condition fluctuated and he had several heart attacks. Elsie Cowan kept on praying to Swami, and finally Walter was declared to be perfectly all right, hale and hearty with no trace of his previous ailments. Discharged from the hospital, the Cowan couple proceeded to Bangalore and stayed in a hotel. Walter

Cowan's Bangalore physician conducted his own laboratory tests and found that all tests were negative. Swami was at that time at Brindavanam, Whitefield and John Hislop, too, was there. Swami sent a message to the Cowans through John Hislop that Walter Cowan should visit Whitefield ashram in day time and return to the hotel to take proper rest. John Hislop comments:

> The extraordinary thing seems to be that, when the total organism that was Walter Cowan died; the only entity that returned to life was Walter himself. Walter's various diseases died with him, but the diseases were not reborn; only Walter was reborn. A most marvellous and inscrutable event, is it not? All of the foregoing does not, of course, imply that Walter's physical body had become immortal. Of course he has had some bad days. At times, he has become overtired, and at times has suffered perhaps because of an injudious meal. After all, it is not a teen-aged body; it is an aged body, but nevertheless a great miracle really happened.
>
> Walter is alive again, free of disease and filled with enthusiasm to tell people about the Divine presence of Sri Sathya Sai Baba.
>
> (John Hislop, Quoted by Elsie Cowan, 'Sai Baba and the Resurrection of Walter Cowan', S.P. Ruhela ed., *Sai Baba and His Message,* p. 236)

Further to celebrate the occasion of Walter Cowan's resurrection, the couple were blessed by Baba and united in wedding ceremony which is clear evidence of Baba's great love for the couple. To give further credence to this miraculous event Walter Cowan has himself related his unique experience. He says:

> While in the Connemara hotel in Madras, two days after I arrived, I was taken very sick with pneumonia and was in bed. As I gasped for breath, suddenly the body's struggle was over and I died. I found myself very calm, in a state of wonderful bliss, and the Lord, Sai Baba, was by my side. Even though my body lay on the bed, dead, my mind kept working throughout until Baba brought me back. There was no anxiety or fear, but a tremendous sense of well being, for I had lost all fear of death.

Baba took me to a large hall where there were hundreds of people milling round. It was a hall where all of the records of all my lives were kept. Baba and I stood before the court Justice. The one in charge knew Baba very well and he asked for the records of all my lives. He was very nice and kind, and I had the feeling that whatever was decided would be the best for my soul. The records were brought into the hall —armloads of scrolls—and all of them seemed to be in different languages. As they were read, Baba interpreted them. In the beginning they told me of countries that have not existed for thousands of years, and I could not recall them. When they reached King David, the readings of my lives became more exciting. I could hardly believe how great I apparently was in each life that followed. As they continued reading my lives, it seemed that what really counted was my motives and character, as I stood for outstanding peace and spirituality. I do not remember all the names, but I am included in almost all of the history books from the beginning of time. As I incarnated in different countries, I carried out my mission—which was peace and spirituality.

After about two hours, they finished reading the scrolls and the Lord, Sai Baba, said that I had not completed the work that I was born to do, and he asked the Judge that I be turned over to him to complete the mission of spreading Truth and he requested that my soul be returned to the body under Baba's Grace. The Judge said, 'So be it!' The case was dismissed and I left with Baba to return to my body. I hesitated to leave this wonderful bliss, but I knew it was best to complete my mission so that I could merge with the Lord, Sai Baba. I related the story to Elsie at once, and she recorded it. I also talked it over to Baba, and he said it was not my imagination—it was a true experience. My life goes on now under the Grace of Sai Baba, whom I adore and to whom I owe my life.

(Walter R. Cowan, S.P. Ruhela ed., *op. cit.*)

Samuel Sandweiss writes:

After Hislop had heard Walter give this account he asked

Sai Baba whether Walter's experience was real or some sort of hallucination. Baba replied: 'The experience was a real experience, not an illusion. It was an experience occurring within Mr. Cowan's mind and I myself was there—directing and clarifying the thoughts.' When asked if every person has similar experience with death, Baba said it is not necessarily so, some may have similar experiences, some not.

(*Sai Baba: The Holy Man and the Psychiatrist*, p. 103)

Baba is the dispenser of all boons, the Absolute sole Lord of life and death. It was chiefly on account of his love for the Cowan couple, their nobility and purity of heart and soul that he brought Walter Cowan back to life from the world of the dead. And actually, the resurrected Walter Cowan lived for some more time engaged in his mission to spread peace and spirituality, doing the work for Baba. And we have it on record that when Walter passed away a few years later that Baba sent word to Elsie Cowan: 'Walter has reached safely' which implied that Walter's yearning to merge with Sai Baba had been fulfilled.

Not only in the power of divinity to resurrect people from not only the brink of death, but also from actual death, the death of the body, there is a great deal of similarity between Sai Baba and Jesus of Nazareth. As for the outstanding and breath-taking miracles, instances are too many and can be cited both from the Bible and from the authentic biography of Baba and from the countless number of accounts given by close devotees of Sai Baba. The present author has witnessed and even experienced the working of such miracles and has been the recipient of the Grace of Sai Baba which has effected a sea-change in his life and has brought a new and sustaining vision of the divine essence incarnated in Sri Sathya Sai Baba.

Sai Baba, like Jesus Christ, is a Ray from the Supreme. Incarnations, like Krishna, Christ and Sai Baba, come after epochs. The event of their coming marks the end of the sad, waste time, the degeneration of moral and spiritual values and the beginning of a new age. Krishna, the full incarnation, lived five thousand years ago and directed humanity to the pathways of peace and love. Jesus Christ came two thousand years ago. He brought the kingdom of the heaven on earth both by his teachings and by his own example. Sai Baba has a more difficult and challenging task as he has come in an age of rank scepticism and eclipse of all moral and spiritual values. But he has declared, time and again, that the task for which he has come, will succeed and the golden age would dawn upon the earth. He says: 'My life is my message.'

Another striking similarity between Sai Baba and Jesus Christ has to do with the preaching of sermons. The commandments of Jesus Christ and his teachings, specially delivered in the Sermon on the Mount contain the series of illuminations which are as sacred as Holy Writ. The teachings have reached vast millions of Christians all over the world and have made Christianity the most universal and effective of all religions. The central kernel of Christ's teaching is the emphasis on love, faith and charity. Not that there is something entirely new, original and revolutionary in his sermons; they consist of, and are the concentrated essence of the eternal verities contained in all world religions, including Hinduism and Buddhism. One can find a close resemblance between teachings of the Vedas, Upanishads, *Shastras* and *Purans* and the gospel of Christ. It has been substantiated that Christ had visited India and was conversant fully with Indian thought and philosophy. Sai Baba has thrown an altogether new light on the life of Christ. And he has even gone on saying that there was a deep relationship between him and Jesus. The remaining portion of this chapter will deal with this aspect of the close affinity between the two, as between father and son. Sai Baba emphasizes the central unity of all religions. He says: There is only one caste, the caste of humanity. There is only one religion, the religion of love. There is only one God and he is omnipresent.

This essential unity of all religions is revealed by the logo seen at the *Ashram*. The symbols of the five major world religions appear in the logo. They are 'Aum of Hinduism', the 'Wheel of Buddhism', the 'Fire of Zoroastrianism', the 'Cross of Christianity' and the 'Crescent and Star of Islam'. The symbolic meanings of these symbols reveal and demonstrate the eternal verities of life and man's burden of the spiritual quest.

Listen to the primeval Aum resounding in your heart as well as in the heart of the universe; Remember the Wheel of Cause and Consequence, of deed and destiny and the Wheel of *Dharma* that fights them all; Offer all bitterness to the sacred Fire and emerge grand, great and Godly; Cut the 'I' feeling clean across and let your ego die on the Cross to endow on you eternity; Be like the Star which never wavers from the Crescent and is ever fixed in steady faith. The main thrust and purpose of all religions is to make present in man his intrinsic and innate humaneness and to take him to the heights of divinity. Religion, in the ultimate analysis, is to enable man to get over alienation from man, nature and God and to help him get over his loneliness.

It seems Sai Baba considers Jesus Christ to be very dear to him. The very fact that Christmas is celebrated at Prasanthi Nilayam is a clear pointer of his partiality towards the Christians. Although the devotees of Baba belong generally to all the major religions of the world, the single largest groups are the followers of Hinduism and Christianity. However, the followers of Islam are seen in microscopic minority although some of the sincere and resilient ones belong to that religion.

Returning to the theme of the title of this chapter, 'Sai Baba and Jesus of Nazareth'. In their beautiful and exciting book, *Sai Baba: The Embodiment of Love,* referring to Sai Baba's Christmas discourse of 1972, Ron Lang asked Sai Baba the following question in an interview given by Sai Baba in January 1980: 'Does this omission in the Bible mean it was you who sent Jesus of Nazareth into incarnation?' 'Yes', he replied. Ron Lang continues, 'My wife and I gasped, although I have no recollection of this. Followed my question: which lay at the very core of my soul: in that case, are you what Western Christians call the Cosmic Christ?' 'Yes', he replied.

(Kailash Kumar and Jorgan Hovegaard, *Sai Baba: The Source of Light, Love and Bliss*, p. 88)

In the words of Ron Lang,

> As the reader can imagine, my wife and I came out of that interview in a daze. So Sathya Sai Baba was the one whom Jesus called the Father, the Christ indeed, the Cosmic Christ.

> The second coming had come, had lived for forty-four years on earth and perhaps only a handful of Christians were aware of it. At first, it was too stupendous to grasp. Yet I only know that I came to believe it, and I am reporting precisely what happened.
>
> (Ron Lang and Peggy Mason, *Sai Baba: The Embodiment of Love,* p. 40)

In his Christmas day discourse in 1972 he had given some more valuable and revealing information about Jesus Christ. He said:

> There is one point that I cannot but bring to your special notice today. At the moment when Jesus was emerging in the Supreme principle of Divinity, he communicated some news to his followers, which has been interpreted in a variety of ways by commentators, and those who relish the piling of writings on writings and meanings on meanings, until it all swells up into a huge mess.
>
> The statement itself has been manipulated and tangled into a conundrum. The statement of Christ is simple: 'He who sent me among you will come again.' And he pointed to a lamb. The lamb is merely a symbol, a sign. It stands for the voice 'Ba-Ba' — the announcement was of the advent of Baba. 'His name will be Truth,' Christ declared. Sathya means Truth. 'He will wear a robe of red, a blood red robe. (Here Baba pointed to the robe he was wearing.) He will be short, with a crown of hair.' The lamb is the sign and symbol of love. Christ did not declare that he will come again. He said, 'He who made me will come again. That Ba-Ba is this Baba and Sai, the short curly-hair crowned red-robed Baba, is come. He is not only in this form, but in everyone of you, as the dweller of the heart. He is there, short, with a robe of the colour of blood that fills it.'
>
> (Quoted by Kailash Kumar, *op. cit.,* p. 89)

Like Jesus of Nazareth, Sai Baba, too, is a Ray from the Supreme, a symbol perfected in love. In another discourse in 1972, Baba said:

> People talk of the sacrifice of Christ as evidenced by his crucifixion. But he was surrounded and bound, and crowned by the crowd who captured him with a crown of thorns and later nailed to the cross by his captors. A person bound and beaten by the police cannot say that he has sacrificed anything, for he is not a free man. Let us pay attention to the sacrifices that Jesus made while free out of his own volition. He sacrificed his happiness, his prosperity, comfort, safety and position. He braved the enmity of the powerful. He renounced the ego, which is the toughest thing to get rid of. Honour him for these. He willingly sacrificed the desires with which the body torments man, this is sacrifice greater than the sacrifice of the body under duress.
>
> (Quoted by Kailash Kumar, *op. cit.*, pp. 87-88)

There cannot be any better and more revealing commentary on the supreme sacrifice made by Jesus, that is the renunciation of everything and the final embrace of death and martyrdom so that mankind could live and attain the kingdom of heaven. In this sense, the crucifixion of Christ may be regarded as a supreme act of love and self-surrender. Only the divine which is truly the embodiment of love could lay down his life for the good of mankind. Love is chief motivating force behind the actions of an *Avatar*. Sai Baba has not hitched his wagon to the stars; he has started his mission to bring all humanity together under evangel news of universal brotherhood of man and the fatherhood of God. According to him God is love and Love is God. Thus, all the three major incarnations of God, Krishna, Christ and Sathya Sai Baba are truly symbols perfected in love.

Jesus Christ also centres his sermons and teachings on the sublimating and unifying principle of love. 'Love thy neighbour as thyself.' There is equal emphasis on charity, compassion, faith and forgiveness which are the central gems which Christianity is all about. Christ says: 'The kingdom of heaven is within you.' Baba also stresses the idea that there is the inner divinity in all of us and the whole purpose of the spiritual quest or *sadhana* is to merge oneself with *parmatma,* Being, Awareness and Bliss. A close look at Christ's *Sermon on the Mount* and Sai Baba's insistence on four quartets of moral values or the gems of golden ray serene as discussed in the next chapter, bear as close a resemblance, almost one to one correspondence between Baba and Jesus of Nazareth. However, it must be clearly borne in mind that neither Jesus in his time nor Sathya Sai Baba today has said anything very original or revolutionary. These are the eternal verities dear to all religions but in the life of Jesus of Nazareth and in that of Sri Sathya Sai Baba they acquire a particular power and intensity because they are sincerely believed in and arise out of the realized experiences of the *Avatars*. Sai Sathya Sai Baba has declared unequivocally that he had come to establish *sanatana dharma* the eternal religion and to repair the ancient highway to God. Both Jesus and Sai Baba have set their own examples. Jesus said, for example: 'I am the way, the truth and the life.' And further he said: 'I am the bread of life. I am the light of the world. I am the way, the truth and the life.' Sai Baba asks people to emulate Christ and follow the ideals dear to him. In his discourse on the Christmas of 1978, Baba said:

> Jesus was a master born with a purpose. The mission of restoring Love, Charity and Compassion in the heart of man. He had no attachment to the self; he never paid heed to sorrow or pain; joy or gain; he had a heart that responded to the call of anguish, the cry for peace and Brotherhood. He went about the land preaching the lesson of love and poured out his life as a libation in the sacrifice to humanity... From the attitude of being a messenger of God he declared that he was the son of God, after returning from the East. For the old attitude meant duality, a master-servant relationship. One had to carry out the duties laid down by the Master, and in the Scriptures of faith. This he found too irksome and felt he was the image, while God was the original. The bond of relationship increased: The 'I' was no longer in some distant light or entity, the light became a part of the 'I'. Jesus could declare: 'I and my Father are one.' Just as one states: I was in the Light, then, the Light was in me, and now, I am aware that I am the Light.
>
> (Quoted by Krishna Kumar, *op. cit.*, pp. 86-87)

Thus, it becomes increasingly clear that Sri Sathya Sai Baba has clear conception of the life and message of Jesus Christ, as indeed he has of all other *Avatars.* This is so because he represents the same divine principle and is the same Divine and Ultimate essence which is known as God Almighty. One is, therefore, not surprised that he has disclosed material and information about Jesus Christ not available in the Holy Bible. And he has also given a positive answer to the query of Ron Lang that it was He who had sent Jesus and that he was what the Western Christians called Cosmic Christ.

In reality, Sri Sathya Sai Baba believes in the unity of all religions, all faiths and beliefs and in the immanence of one God who is omnipresent. There are different facets of an *Avatar*. He comes with requisite powers to be able to accomplish the chosen task. This power is transcendental, all-pervasive and universal. This author firmly believes that the *Avatar,* may he be Krishna, Jesus Christ or Sathya Sai Baba, is a Ray Supreme from the eternal Absolute and he comes at the intersection point between Time and Eternity. He is at the spring and source of all knowledge and can pick up knowledge from the vast storehouse of knowledge by virtue of his universal omniscience. He knows the past, present and future of everyone and is perfectly capable of dispensing rewards and punishment, depending on the *karma* of the subject.

This author had the privilege of reading *Ramkatha Rasvahini* and has found material about the life of Rama not found in either Valmiki *Ramayana* or *Ramcharit Manas* written by Tulsidas. This author also recalls his presence at an informal meeting of teachers of Sri Sathya Sai Institute of Higher Learning. It was a very enlightened and knowledgeable audience. One of the eminent devotees, a former Vice Chancellor of Benares Hindu University, requested Swami to give a discourse on the life of the great saint Tulsidas who wrote *Ramcharit Manas* which has swayed millions of people through centuries and is also a devotional work *par excellence*. Swami gave a vivid and graphic description of the life and career of that immortal writer and a devotee of the highest class and calibre. That account was perfect and flawless as Swami knew all about his one-time great devotee. So, there is no wonder that the hidden facts about Christ's life and career, his actions and motivations were readily available to Swami. Time and space is of no consequence to him and he can *know* all in a flash. In this context, the author would relate yet another example. A visitor from the Ministry of Education, Government of India, who happened to be a specialist in the modern concept of preparing question banks for the overall benefit of the students in colleges and universities, came to discuss the idea of preparing question bank at the deemed university. He addressed the teachers and took them in confidence. This is what he said as a preamble to his address: "You will doubtless be surprised to know that I have had a personal interview with Swami this morning. He seemed to know the purpose of my visit and discussed the subject in detail. I said to myself 'He may be a great saint or a mystic, fully conversant with religious texts; what would he know about the modern reforms in education and the idea and necessity of having question banks.' So, sceptically I listened to him, and was wonder-struck to find that not only he knew what was in my mind and thought, but all that had been written and spoken on the subject by the great specialists on the subject. Really and truly He is the speaker of all words, thinker of all thoughts, doer of all deeds."

I would like to close this chapter by relating yet another exciting aspect of Sri Sathya Sai Baba, namely, his materialization of an image of Jesus Christ on the Cross with the minutest details of his face and feeling, which might well be rated as the finest piece of sculpture. Swami has told John Hislop that there was some delay in the materialization as after a lapse of thousands of years it was a problem finding the wood on which Jesus Christ was nailed. This is how Dr. Samuel Sandweiss narrates the whole episode:

> ...There is the very unusual story told by Dr. John Hislop—a close devotee of Baba. Breaking two twigs off a tree and placing them together in the form of a cross, he asked John what they looked like and John replied that they looked like a cross. Baba then placed the twigs in his hand, blew on them three times and opened his hand to reveal a wooden Cross with a silver statue of Jesus on it. He said that the statue was not simply an artist's representation of Jesus but

an exact likeness of how he actually looked on the Cross. The small crucifix on which the silver statue was mounted, he said, was taken from Christ's actual Cross.

This is Dr. Hislop's account.

Baba, a large group of students from the Sathya Sai Arts and Science College at Brindavan and a few other people, including myself were walking down the bank of a road to a stretch of level sand of the dry Kekkanahalla river bed. I was walking alongside Swami, and as we passed a bush, he reached over and pulled off a couple of twigs, and held them up like a Cross. Hislop, he said, what is this?

'Well, Swami, it is a Cross,' I answered. He put the twigs in his hand, closed it, and produced rather three slow breaths on it. Then he opened his hand and gave me a cross with figure of Christ on it. This is an image of Christ on the cross, he said — not as artists have imagined him and as historians have told about him, but as he actually and truly was, with stomach pulled away in and ribs all showing because he had no food for eight days.

So, I said, 'Well the cross, Swami, tell me about that.'

'The Cross is a piece of wood from the original on which Christ was crucified. Then he said something very interesting: 'To find a piece of that wood after two thousand years presented a little difficulty.' I suppose, that is why he breathed rather slowly three times. Usually, he gives one puff, and a ring or whatever does appear.

I noticed something odd and asked, 'Swami, what is that hole at the top of cross?'

He replied, 'That is the hole where they hung the cross on the standard.' This is something we had not even heard of before. Pictures of Christ being crucified show the cross being planted on the ground; but according to Swami, it was hung on something, and you can actually see the hole in the wood. My wife and I were absolutely astounded. I am sure it is the greatest sculpture of Christ that has ever been made. You can see the blood flowing from his forehead. You can see the black and dust-caked saliva at the corner of his mouth. The expression of agony, pain and suffering in his eyes and face will tear your heart, and show the beauty of the tiny figure of Christ. In my estimation, it is the most extraordinary object that Baba has ever produced. When Walter Woolf brought some enlargements of the photograph down to our house, we were standing around the table looking at the pictures and thinking of Christ and of Baba, when suddenly, from a perfectly clear sky there was a terrible crash of thunder. Then a very strong wind blew through the house, rattling the shutters, banging the doors and blowing the curtains. Next day, an article in *San Diego Tribune* reported that mysterious thunder and wind had come up unexpectedly from a perfectly clear sky. My wife reminded me that Christ died on the cross at five O'clock and that the Bible tells us of thunder and earthquake which arose suddenly. I can only conclude that there is a tremendous amount of power in that little cross.

(Quoted by Samuel Sandweiss, *Sai Baba: The Holy Man and the Psychiatrist*, pp. 175-76)

So, the relationship between Sri Sathya Sai Baba and Jesus of Nazareth is deeper and more intrinsic and vital than we generally imagine. The fact that he materializes talismans like the picture and statue of Christ by the simple wave of the hand and offers them to his Christian devotees is common knowledge. Not only this, he generally exhorts the audiences to follow the teachings of Jesus Christ and live by them. And on that fateful Christmas day in 1972, he was pleased to say the last word on the subject which has the sanction and weight of a revelation, as it were. As already testified by Ron Lang and Peggy Mason in their book, *Sai Baba: The Embodiment of Love*: Christ said, 'He who has sent me will come again' and that Ba-Ba — the symbol of the voice of lamb is this Baba, short, hair-crowned, red robe Baba come again.

So, the implication of the Second Coming has been finally cleared and resolved by none else than Baba himself, and one feels that the vision of terror transmitted by William Butler Yeats in his well known poem, *The Second Coming,* suggesting the coming of a huge monster, struggling to be born at Bethleham, was just a delusion. Actually, at a time when the ceremony of innocence is drowned and the good lack all conviction and the worst are full of passionate intensity, the coming of the *Avatar* is the natural consequence. In that famous Christmas day discourse, Baba told the audience:

> And the story says there was a star in the sky which fell with a new light, and this led a few and others to the place where the saviour was born. This story is read and taken on trust by man, though stars do not fall or even slide down so suddenly. What the story signifies is this: There was a huge aura of splendour illumining the sky over the village where Christ was born. This meant that He who was to overcome the darkness of evil and ignorance had taken birth, that He would spread the light of love in the heart of man and the councils of humanity. Appearances of splendour or of other signs are natural of the era that has dawned when incarnations happen on earth.
>
> (*Sanatana Sarathi,* April 1975)

When questioned by an interviewer, Dr. Samuel Sandweiss, the renowned psychiatrist who acquired a new vision of reality and an insight into what truly matters in the spiritual quest and destiny of man, said:

> Q. What is Baba's relationship with Christ?
>
> A. This is a very interesting question. I have mentioned before he has said that he is all names and all forms, that he and Christ or any form or embodiment of God, are the same. But he has drawn the connection between Christ and himself in a number of very interesting ways.
>
> (Samuel Sandweiss, *op. cit.,* p. 174)

And furthermore,

> On April 20, 1972 while seated among a small group of devotees — American devotees — Sai Baba reportedly performed a miracle which more than words could points out the connection between Christ, Shiva and himself. The

> devotees said that by a wave of his hand he materialized this small medallion picturing Jesus on its surface. The tiny medallion was passed from person to person through the group of devotees for everyone to examine. Taking it back into his hand, Baba blew on it twice transforming the image on the surface, according to those present, to that of Lord Shiva.
>
> (Samuel Sandweiss, *op. cit.*, p. 172)

Thus it is clear that Sri Sathya Sai Baba, Christ and Lord Shiva represent the same divinity and that there is absolutely no difference between them. In fact, many devotees have had the experience of seeing their own favourite and chosen God when they have cast their glance on the frail, red-robed figure of Sri Sathya Sai Baba. This is not just a *maya* or Illusion. But when one is in the presence of an *Avatar,* he is face to face with God and our notion of reality undergoes a sea-change. However, the perceptions of the individual depend largely on his own personal and individual stage of development in the realm of the spirit. Many Christians have been drawn to the orbit of Baba's influence only after they have gone through authentic and convincing proofs. So we come to the end of this chapter with the positive and firm conclusion that there is only one God and that he is omnipresent. The followers of different religions see him in different names and forms though he is essentially the same Divine force and energy, the same blazing Light, the Ray Supreme. The sameness of different names and forms has to be discerned only by the advanced and discerning aspirant. Sri Sathya Sai Baba has rightly declared that he is *Sarva-devata-swarup,* the quintessence of all names and forms of God. He has further said:

> I am not Sathya Sai Baba. It is only a name by which you know me today. All names are mine. I am the one God who answers the prayers that rise in human hearts in all languages from all countries addressed to all forms of deity.
>
> (Sathya Sai Baba)

5

THE PERPETUAL STAR AT SHIRDI

Sri Sathya Sai Baba, who has made the unique revelation about the relationship between Jesus Christ and himself on the Christmas day of 1972, has chosen to make another important revelation. This time about the *Sai Avatar* on September 28, 1990. Little was known about Sai Baba, particularly about his birth and childhood and his nascent divinity before he had landed at Shirdi in 1858 with the Barat party of Chandu Patel's brother's son.

When R.K. Karanjia asked what made him so sure that he was Shirdi Baba incarnate, Sri Sathya Sai Baba said:

> The knowledge of my own authentic experience, of course. Since no one who knew Shirdi Baba is alive today, there is no evidence except my own knowledge and experience. The very fact that I announced that I am Shirdi Baba forty years ago, when I was only 10 and nobody in this part of the South had known or even heard of Shirdi Baba, proves the fact.

(Samuel Sandweiss, *Spirit and the Mind,* p. 238)

Sri Sathya Sai Baba on September 28, 1990, made the dramatic disclosure about the facts hitherto unknown about the advent of the first Sai Avatar at Shirdi, Maharashtra, and the fact that he himself was the reincarnation of Sai Baba in human form as prophesied by Sai Baba in a talk with some of his close devotees. He said:

> I propose today to reveal what has not been known to anyone hitherto. In the former Nizam's dominions, there was a remote village called Pathri. In that village there were a couple named Gangabhavadiya and Devagiriamma. They

were grieving over lack of children. In answer to their prayer, a son was born on September 28, 1835. Today is the anniversary of that day. That child was Sai Baba. September 28th was the date of his birth. On Vijayadashmi day in 1918, he gave up his body.

When Gangabhavadiya and Devagiriamma were living in Pathri village, they were worshippers of Iswara and Parvati. They had no offspring for a long time. Gangabhavadiya used to ply boats near the village for a living. One night when it was raining heavily, Gangabhavadiya left his house to take care of the boats, telling his wife that he would not be returning in the night. After the husband had left, she ate and went to bed at 9 P.M. There was a knock at the door. Devagiriamma opened the door, expecting the return of her husband. A very old man entered the house. He pleaded, 'It is very cold outside. Please permit me, mother, to stay inside.' As a pious woman, she allowed him to stay inside in the verandah and went in after bolting the inner door. A little while later, there was a knock on the inner door. She opened the door. The old man said, 'I am feeling hungry; give me some food.' Finding that there was no food, the woman mixed some flour with curd and gave it to him. There was again another knock after some time. When she opened the door, the old man said, 'My legs are aching. Mother, will you massage them?' Devagiriamma went inside, sat in the prayer room, and prayed: 'Oh mother, why are you testing me like this? What should I do? Should I serve him or refuse?' Going out of the house by the back door, she went in search of someone who could be engaged to render help to the old man. At the same time, a woman knocked at the back door. She said, 'It appears you came to my house and sought some feminine help. I was away at that time. Please tell me what service should I render?' Feeling happy that Goddess Parvathi herself had sent the woman in response to her prayers, Devagiriamma sent the woman to the verandah for serving the old man and closed the door. The old man and the new woman were none other than Parameshwara and Parvathi, the divine couple.

Parameshwara told Parvathi: 'Fulfil the cherished desires of this lady.' Parvathi told Eswara, 'You are the Supreme, please shower your grace on her yourself.' Eswara said, 'I came to test her. You came in answer to the prayers. Hence you must bless her.' There was a knock at the door again. This time Devagiriamma opened the door because of the presence of another woman there. Parvathi and Parameshwara appeared before her in their divine form. Unable to control her joy, Devagiriamma fell at their feet. Parvathi then blessed her, 'I grant you a son to maintain the lineage and a daughter for *kanyadan* (a girl to offer in marriage).'

Then she fell at the feet of Eswara. Eswara said: 'I am immensely pleased with your devotion. I shall take birth as your third child.' When Devagiriamma got up, the divine couple were not there. Feeling ecstatic over this experience Devagiriamma was eagerly expecting the return of her husband in the morning to relate to him the whole story. He returned in the morning. Eagerly she related to him all that had happened the previous night. He husband said, 'Devagiri, what is all this fanciful tale? It is all a dream. Parvathi and Parameshwara appearing before you and giving *Darshan*! It is pure fantasy.' Gangabhavadiya dismissed the whole episode as incredible and fanciful.

But as years passed Devagiriamma became pregnant and a son was born. A year later a daughter was born. Gangabhavadiya was convinced that the birth of the two children was the result of the blessing conferred by Parvathi and Parameshwara. When she conceived again, Gangabhavadiya began to feel an urge to give up home and hearth and go in search of the divine couple. He announced to his wife that he was leaving for the forest to do penance. The devoted wife that she was, she decided to follow him, though she was in the ninth month of pregnancy. After proceeding some distance, she developed labour pains. She was delivered of a boy. Wrapping the baby in a piece of cloth she left the child by the roadside and followed her husband. Because of this circumstance no one knew who the parents were. Baba's life story is known only after his arrival in Shirdi.

There was in the same village a Sufi *Fakir*. As he was also childless he took charge of the child and brought him up in his home. The boy stayed at the *Fakir's* home for four years. The *Fakir* passed away in the tide of time. The *Fakir's* wife who had lavished great affection on the child, was grief-stricken. To add further to her worries the boy was behaving in a troublesome manner. In those days Hindu-Muslim differences in that area were growing alarmingly. There was considerable bitterness among members of the two communities. What the boy used to do was to visit a Hindu temple and sing songs in praise of Allah: 'Mein Allah hoon', 'Allah malik hai' (Allah is the supreme Lord). He used to declare in this manner in the temple. Not only that, but he would enter a mosque and declare 'Rama is God', 'Shiva is Allah'. His behaviour in singing about Allah in a Hindu temple and about Rama and Shiva in a mosque was a puzzle to the public. Members belonging to both the communities went to the Fakir's wife and complained about the boy's behaviour.

Unable to deal with this situation the Fakir's wife handed over the boy to a pious scholar named Venkusa who was living near the house. One night in 1858 the boy left the *Ashram*. He reached Shirdi a very small village at that time. He stayed there for two months and then went about wandering from place to place. After strolling for many years, he reached a place called Dhoopkheda. When he was residing there, the marriage of Chandu Patel's brother's son was celebrated there. Baba joined the marriage party and reached Shirdi again which was in the year 1858. From that day till 1918 he did not move out of Shirdi. He remained there for sixty years. While at Shirdi, Baba used to converse with those coming to him, give advice to them regarding their problems. In this manner Baba's activities came to be known all over the country. In 1917 Baba called Nanachandorkar Mahalsa-Pathi, Abdul Baba and Dasgabe and others and started asking each of them, 'Do you know who you are?' Each of them replied, 'I am your *sishya* (Disciple).' Baba said, 'Nonsense! Don't use that term any longer I have no disciples in this world. I have countless devotees. Do you recognize the difference between a disciple and a devotee? Anyone can be a devotee, but that is not the case with a disciple. A disciple is one who carries out implicitly the commands of the Guru (The Preceptor). The mark of a *sishya* is total devotion to the Preceptor. Only the man who says I have none in the world other than the preceptor is a disciple. How far have you respected my injunctions? How are you entitled to claim that you are a disciple? Only the one who follows me like my shadow can claim to be my disciple. The devotee is one who prays to the Lord wherever he may be. Hence there is a difference between a devotee and a disciple. The disciple and the preceptor are like two bodies with one spirit. The disciple should have no sense of separation from the preceptor. He should feel 'I and you are one'. There are millions of devotees but no disciple.'

All that Baba said or did was for the good of the devotees alone. Towards the end, Abdul Baba came to Baba. Baba told him, 'I shall appear again and give you *darshan*.'

'When will that be?' asked Abdul Baba and was told, 'It will be after eight years.'

'The first advent of Sai was in Maharashtra. The second advent will be in Madras,' Baba said. It should be noted that when this form (Sathya Sai) made its advent, Andhra Pradesh was part of Madras Presidency.

When he was asked in what form the next advent would take place, Shirdi Baba told Abdul Baba, 'I will give *darshan* in the name of Sathya for upholding truth.' That is the present advent.

The two bodies are different, but the Divinity is one—the first advent was for revealing Divinity. The second one is to awaken Divinity (in human beings).

The next advent is for propagating Divinity. The three Sais are Shirdi Sai, Sathya Sai, and Prema Sai. The reason for relating all this is that today happens to be birthday of Shirdi Baba. Baba attained *samadhi* in 1918. Bodies are transient.

> These vestures are assumed only for the sake of devotees. Unless the Divine comes with a form, no one can develop faith in the formula. The Divine in human form is the preparation for comprehending the formulae absolute.
>
> The truth about God cannot be understood by anyone. He is infinitely vast. He is minuter than atom. No one can know what is the macrocosm and what is microcosm? It is not easy for anyone to understand the ways of the Lord. When one cannot understand the ways of the Divine, it is best to keep silent and at least refrain from indulging in grievous misinterpretation. Seek, therefore, to understand the ways of God and through devotion and worship strive to experience the Divine.
>
> (Sathya Sai Baba, Discourse on September 28, 1990, Quoted by R.T. Kakade *et al., Shirdi to Puttaparthi,* pp. 79-83)

Sri Sathya Sai Baba has said that at the time of the advent of Jesus Christ a star broke away from the heaven and this phenomenon was observed by some Tibetans and others. Although a star does not actually break from the Empyreon, it is symbolic of the birth of an incarnation on earth, transmitting waves of supernatural light, aura and splendour. When Sai Baba was born and wrapped in piece cloth was placed by the roadside by his mother Devagiriamma no supernatural phenomenon was witnessed by anyone nor any aura or splendour was visible. However, we have the story about the vision in which the proud mother saw Shankar and Parvathi and was bestowed the divine boon that Parameswara would himself take birth as the third child of the devoted couple. The abandoned child was picked up by a *Sufi* Fakir named Patil and was bred and brought up by him and his wife. But as an *Avatar* is destined to reveal his splendour in fulfilment of the *Avataric* design, the child, Babu as he was called by the Fakir's wife, did show his infinite splendour even as Lord Krishna had shown to his foster mother Yashoda. This is how it happened in the words of Professor Gokak:

> One day, the boy was playing at marbles with the son of a neighbouring Sahukar or wealthy man. The Sahukar's son lost all his marbles to Babu. Tempted by the game, the Sahukar's

son went to his mother's worship room, seized a *saligram* or a black globular stone and played with it as a marble. The Sahukar's son lost that *saligram* also to Babu. The Sahukar's son went to his mother and told her that Babu had played foul and that the *saligram* should be returned to him. Babu refused to part with it. He kept it in his mouth. When the Sahukar's wife, a devout and pious woman devoted to Lord Shiva, came to know about it, she was horrified. She rushed to her worship room and found to her dismay that the *saligram* was actually missing. She ran to the spot where Babu was playing with her son and importuned him to return the *saligram.* Babu remained tight-lipped and refused to return the *saligram.* She then compelled him to open his mouth and saw in it what Yashoda had seen in Sri Krishna's—the *vishwaroop,* worlds rolling on worlds. But no *saligram.* Babu laughingly said that the *saligram* was in her worship room. She ran back there and found the *saligram.* She came back to Babu and prostrated herself before him. She had now realised that he was Divine.

(V.K. Gokak, *Sai Baba: Man and Avatar,* p. 64)

Sai Baba was no doubt the universal master and one of the greatest and finest saints that India has ever produced. More than that, he was the God who walked the earth to sow the seeds of secular integration and universal brotherhood. Attempts have been made by some biographers and devotees to present a true interpretation of his divinity in concrete terms. John Osborne's *'The Incredible Sai'* is one such attempt. In fact, there is the existence of what is commonly designated as Sai Baba movement in India. Most of the social and cultural historians view Sai Baba of Shirdi as a vital link, a promoter, not an inaugurator of the Sai Baba movement that owes its beginning and true ancestry to the medieval poet and saint, Kabir. Born in the fifteenth century, the greatest contribution of Kabir was to bring about reformation in Hindu asceticism and in creating a link between Hindus and Muslims. It is not known for certain whether he was born a Hindu or Muslim. Now the accepted opinion is that he was a Hindu by choice and a theist, he taught an extreme form of devotion to the God without qualities. He also referred to the

God of his inner experience as his Guru. Kabir's humble origins, his love for all mankind, whether Hindu, Muslim or otherwise and his great love and compassion for animals, his yogic connections with the *Nathpanthi* order of saints and his synthetic belief in the unity of all religions point the direction towards the founder of the Sai Baba movement in India.

Sai Baba of Shirdi has been the most popular of the saints among the masses in central and western India, and his pictures can be found all over the country and there are temples and shrines in his name at Madras, Mangalore, Coimbatore, New Delhi and Bombay. The currency has gained around him as one of the major *Avatars* with great divine powers.

Sai Baba established himself as an incarnation by virtue of his miracles, qualities of omniscience, omnipresence and omnipotence. He used to keep a *dhooni* burning perpetually at Dwarkamai and offered the ash of the *dhooni* to his devotees and sick people who were cured immediately. By means of his miracles, he attracted people to himself and took them forward on the spiritual path. He never asserted that he was the Eternal Absolute, but he said in all humility that he was just a humble servant of Allah and that he could use his influence with Allah to bring about health, wealth and happiness to his devotees. What is strange is that even after he gave up his body on the Vijayadashmi day in 1918, Shirdi has become a place of pilgrimage for many. He is worshipped by millions as a major incarnation, like Rama, Krishna, Vithal, Vithoba and Pandurang. Many devotees have recorded their unique and incredible experiences with Sai Baba of Shirdi, and even those who worshipped him even after his physical manifestation had gone, have been blessed by him. The volume jointly written by Dr. Kakade and Dr. Veerbhadra Rao, entitled *Shirdi to Puttaparthi*, is an instance in point. Some of the sayings of Sai Baba have universal appeal and his injunctions that he will continue to speak from his tomb and that his sincere devotees would not feel the want of anything are widely believed in. The present author's personal experience of visiting Shirdi and stepping into the portals of Dwarkamai, feeling a deep sense of serenity and ineffable bliss that passeth understanding. Standing before the statue of Sai Baba on the hallowed grounds of Shirdi, one realizes that the dead weight of custom, staleness and weariness has been lifted and that one is climbing up the ladders of spiritual ascent. Truly Shirdi appears to be the gateway of heaven. It would be relevant here to quote the eleven sayings of Shirdi Sai Baba in this context.

1. Whoever puts his feet on Shirdi soil, his sufferings would come to an end.
2. The wretched and the miserable would rise to plenty of joy and happiness.
3. I shall be ever active and vigorous even after leaving this earthly body.
4. My tomb shall bless and speak to the needs of my devotees.
5. I shall be active and vigorous even from my tomb.
6. My mortal remains would speak from the tomb.
7. I am ever living to help and guide all who come to me, who surrender to me and who seek refuge in me.
8. If you look to me, I look to you.
9. If you cast your burden on me, I shall surely bear it.
10. If you seek my advice and help, it will be given to you at once.
11. There shall be no want in the house of my devotee.

(Sai Baba of Shirdi, Quoted by R.T. Kakade, p. 11)

Since a detailed account of the life and times of Shirdi Sai Baba is not called for here, it would suffice to say that he was the perpetual star, shining in its resplendent glory and splendour at Shirdi. His resemblance with Kabir is just incidental. One of Sai Baba's favourite term for God Almighty was *Fakir* and the first teacher was a Sufi *Fakir.* As Charles S.J. White rightly points out,

> Moreover, Sai Baba was a celibate, remaining in one place, performing miracles and admonishing his disciples, and keeping a fire perpetually burning at Shirdi. To the functions of a Guru, ascetic and saint, Sai Baba adds that of *Avatar* as many of his devotees and followers consider him as a major

incarnation of this age.

(Charles S.J. White, 'Sai Baba Movement', *Sai Baba and His Message,* ed. S.P. Ruhela *et al.*)

Millions of people throughout the globe consider Sri Sathya Sai Baba as a full and major *Avatar*. However in Western terms, an Avatar is a spiritual teacher and a world redeemer like Christ. Dr. Samuel Sandweiss presents a very rational and altogether convincing definition of the powers and prowess of an incarnation. He says:

> The appearance of an Avatar is an extremely rare and monumental event in the history of mankind; his appeal is universal. He represents the highest expression of man's potential: Consciousness without limit, Love without boundary. He is all power, all love, capable of achieving anything imaginable, a being who dictates history and whose activities benefit all mankind. He is all power. He speaks all languages of the world; is a source of all knowledge, knowing past, present and future; and is in all places at all times. The Avatar's life is a clear sign that will, consciousness and love are the source of all creation—that spirit transcends matter. He is proud of our divine nature.

(Samuel Sandweiss, *Spirit and the Mind,* p. 38)

Certainly, the chief attributes of avatarhood are found in the nature and character of Sai Baba although most of the time, he is hiding himself under a veil and deluding the people by his *maya,* as it were. He often described himself as humble and modest servant of Allah. But there are instances when he has displayed his universal omniscience and omnipresence, assuming different forms and manifesting his presence at different places. He wanted his devotees to be sincere and steadfast in their love and devotion to him and assured them that he would look after all their needs and save them from death, disease and calamities. There was something deeply human and profoundly divine in him that indubitably placed him among the great *avatars*.

Sri Sathya Sai Baba has said that he is the incarnation of Sai Baba of Shirdi, and of course, there is the prophecy made by none other than Lord Shiva to sage Bhardwaja that he himself would incarnate thrice in Kaliyuga, first as Sai Baba at Shirdi, secondly as Sathya Sai Baba as Shiva Shakti at Puttaparthi, and finally as Prema Sai as Shakti at Mandya district of Karnataka. And we have no reason to question or doubt the authenticity of that prophecy. Then we have also the recorded evidence about the vision given to Devagiriamma of village Pathri in Maharashtra that Lord Shiva would appear before her and would take birth as her third child. All these are truly revelations, compounded of fact and fiction, myth, legend and reality so that the whole thing assumes the tenuous character and mystery of a kind that is difficult to understand. It is only through the felt experience of the individual that a clear view of the reality can be apprehended.

Let us, therefore, try to go into the matter concerning the relationship between Sai Baba of Shirdi and Sri Sathya Sai Baba. We have seen how in a personal interview to R.K. Karanjia, Baba clarified the point that he was Sai Baba of Shirdi born again. He said that he knew it from his authentic personal experience as none who lived during the Shirdi incarnation was alive now. However, the experiences of his close devotees amply demonstrate that the two Sais are two bodies and one spirit. If we go through official biography of Sri Sathya Sai Baba, *Sathyam, Shivam, Sundaram* we find a record of the events of 1940 when Sathyanarayan Raju was supposedly bitten by a scorpion and started behaving in a strange fashion. He started declaiming difficult passages in Sanskrit and was taken to village exorcist who subjected him to immense physical torture, shaving his head, scratching it with a razor and putting acid into the cut, and anointing his eyes so that the eyes swelled. Sathyanarayan Raju put up with the ordeal calmly and patiently until he was taken back to Puttaparthi by his parents. But his strange and inexplicable behaviour continued. He produced items like pencil, rubber, toffies and sweets and distributed them among the boys and other onlookers. Greatly incensed by such behaviour of Pedda Venkappa Raju came to him with a rod in his hand and admonished him: 'Tell me who you are, madcap or a God?'

'I am Sai Baba. I have come to ward off your troubles. Keep your houses clean.'

There were very few people in the region who had heard of Sai Baba, the wonder-making mendicant Fakir. However, there was a Government official at the neighbouring town, Penukonda, who happened to be a devotee of Shirdi Sai Baba. Good counsel prevailed and the family took the boy to Penukonda, and hoped that the mystery of his strange behaviour would be cleared. However, the said Government officer did not believe that his great Guru, Shirdi Baba, had reincarnated as a small boy. He dismissed the idea outright and advised the guardians: 'It is mental derangement. The child should be taken to a psychiatric clinic for treatment.'

Here young Sathyanarayan Raju intervened, 'Whose mental derangement? You're just a *pujari*, you can't recognize the very Sai whom you are worshipping.' Saying this, he took a handful of ash from nowhere, threw it in all directions. Earlier at Puttaparthi, when he was pressurized to give concrete evidence that he was Sai Baba, he asked for jasmine flowers and flung them on the floor. The name of Sai Baba was written on the floor by the flowers. Everyone was struck with awe. But the most striking phenomenon was the production of *vibhuti* or sacred ash as if from the fourth dimension in the space that demonstrated the sameness of the two Sais. Shirdi Baba used to keep a fire aflame at Dwarkamai and used the *udi* to bless his devotees. We have it on record that in October 1940 Sathyanarayan Raju renounced the school and the family, saying that he had his work to do and that his devotees were calling him. Thereafter the number of his devotees went on increasing and *bhajans* were sung regularly on Thursdays. Shirdi Baba had also indicated to Abdul Baba that he would give *darshan* again as a boy of fourteen in Andhra Pradesh.

So the identity of the two Sais is established beyond doubt. Shirdi Baba had given up his body in 1918 and Sri Sathya Sai Baba was born on November 23, 1926. And Sathyanarayan Raju's dramatic announcement that he was Sai Baba cannot be brushed aside as mere whim or fancy of a teen-aged boy. Furthermore, Sathyanarayan Raju produced by mere wave of the hand *vibhuti* that was the special trade mark of Shirdi Baba which he used as effective remedy for blessing and curing the serious ailment of his devotees. Moreover, Sathya Sai Baba used to tell his mother that a *Fakir* gave him food to eat when he was refused food by the mother for giving food to the beggars and destitutes.

Professor N. Kasturi has narrated a number of very interesting episodes in the life of Sri Sathya Sai Baba that conclusively prove the identity of the Sai *Avatar*. One such episode is the personal experience of two teachers of Bukkapatnam, who knew Sathya as a student in their school and believed in him. Sathya Sai Baba revealed himself as reincarnation of Shirdi Baba and appeased their curiosity.

The other important and easily verifiable account has to do with the Rani of Chincholi whose husband was an ardent devotee of Shirdi Baba. He used to stay a few months every year at Shirdi. It is also reported by the Rani of Chincholi and her old servants that Shirdi Baba visited Chincholi on occasions and that both the Raja and the visitor used to drive in a *tonga* far out of Chincholi. The Rani of Chincholi came to Puttaparthi in order to see the reincarnation of Shirdi Baba and she was more than convinced that the two Babas were one and the same. Sri Sathya Sai Baba was persuaded to accompany the Rani to Chincholi. There had been many changes in the palace since Shirdi Baba's visit to the place. Sri Sathya Sai Baba at once commented on these changes. He asked what happened to the Margosa tree and to the well around there. He also asked about a stone image which he had given to the Raja as Shirdi Baba long ago. The Rani was not aware of it. However a thorough search was made and the image was found out. One Sri Gayathriswami, a disciple of Shankaracharya of Sringeri, who had spent a year at Shirdi with Shirdi Baba, came to Prasanthi Nilayam to ascertain if Sri Sathya Sai Baba was Shirdi Baba Incarnate. He had a dream one night that Shirdi Baba gave him *darshan* in a dream and said he had returned from his *mahasamadhi* after eight years and that he had brought all his properties with him. Sri Sathya Sai often materializes pictures, rings and other talismans with the imprint of Shirdi Baba's image on them. He also produces the dates from Shirdi and the pieces of Shirdi Baba's *kafni*. Professor Kasturi has related the experience of an incident in which a former devotee is assailed with doubt about the claim of Sathya Sai Baba that he was Shirdi Baba reborn. The devotee while cycling down the road in New Delhi was followed by an old man who asked him to wait for a while near a graveyard off the road and told him all about his work and preoccupations. He further assured him that his Guru was God. Then he stretched his hands and showed both his palms. There were the shining images of Shirdi Baba on one palm and that of Sathya Sai Baba on the other palm. Another incident narrated by Professor Kusturi is of special interest. A lady, a former student of Professor Kasturi and working then as Principal of Devagiri College, Mysore, was sitting on a bench at the Bangalore platform, waiting for the train scheduled to go to Mysore. An old man holding a rod and carrying a box on his head came towards her and finding a seat vacant on the bench by her side engaged in her conversation in Telugu. She told him that she was going over to the mission hospital, Mysore for a surgical operation. The old man who was wearing a *kafni* on his head, advised her not to go in for the operation, as there was absolutely no need for it. Questioned about his identity, the old man said that he was coming from Shirdi and would go back to the same place along with some devotees. He offered her some dates of Shirdi and a packet of *udhi*. Impressed by the aura on the face of the old man, the lady asked him if she could bring some fruits for him. She went to buy some fruits, but when she returned, she found that he was no longer there; only his box was lying on the bench. Later, Sri Sathya Sai Baba told Professor Kasturi that he had met his former student and prevented her from going in for an operation that would have proved fatal. Thus, the resemblance of the old man with Shirdi Baba and his words that he was from Shirdi and was collecting his devotees to take them to Shirdi and, more specially, his offer to the lady of dates from Shirdi and packet of *udhi* make it clear beyond any shadow of doubt that Sathya Sai Baba had assumed the mantle of Shirdi Baba to intervene at a critical moment to save the lady from serious trouble.

Then there is the experience of Mr. M.S. Dixit, the son of Sadashiva Dixit, the elder brother of Hari S. Dixit, a close devotee of Shirdi Baba. M.S. Dixit now lives at Whitefield, Bangalore and has had the unique privilege of being taken to Shirdi by his uncle

Kaka Saheb Dixit where Shirdi Baba had cured him of migraine instantly by just applying the *udhi* on the affected part and asking the disease to go away. This Mr. Dixit came to Prasanthi Nilayam and was called for an interview and went into the room holding a photograph of his uncle Hari S. Dixit in hand. Sri Sathya Sai Baba saw the photograph and recognized him saying 'he is your uncle Hari S. Dixit, my close devotee when I was in my previous body.' Another incredible story is that of a lady who went to Shirdi in 1917 in a state of desolation after the death of her four children and pleaded to Baba that she be allowed to live at Shirdi with him. Baba said, 'Not now. I will come again in Andhra; you will meet me then and be with me.' As the story goes, the said lady, having heard that Shirdi Baba had been born again, went to Urvakonda to see him. Sri Sathya Sai Baba spoke to her softly and affectionately, 'So you have come, my child.' This lady has taken permanent residence at Prasanthi Nilayam. Baba is also reported to have told her that she owed him Sixteen Rupees while he was in his Shirdi manifestation. So the identity of two Sai Babas having different bodies is firmly established. Same divine spirit resided in both.

Sri Sathya Sai Baba has clarified the mystery about his relationship with Shirdi Baba through many beautiful and impressive analogies. Once Sri Sathya Sai said:

> When there are two pieces of candy, one square, another circular, one yellow and the other purple in colour, unless one has eaten and realised the taste of both pieces one cannot believe both. Tasting, experiencing—that is the crucial thing for knowing the identity.
>
> (Sathya Sai Baba, quoted by Howard Murphet, *Man of Miracles,* p. 66)

And furthermore, Sri Sathya Sai differentiates between the two incarnations and their modes of operation:

> The mother is usually hard when the children enter the kitchen and disturb the cooking, but while serving the food she is all smiles and patience. I am now serving the dishes cooked then. Wherever you may be, if you are hungry and

> if your plate is ready, I shall serve you the dishes and will feed you to your heart's content.
>
> (Sathya Sai Baba, quoted by Howard Murphet, *op. cit.*, p. 66)

I have used the metaphor of Perpetual Star in this chapter to symbolise the divine advent of Shirdi Sai Baba who had landed at Shirdi in the nineteenth century and had acquired almost a pan-Indian reputation like Ramkrishna Paramhansa. In my earlier work on Sri Sathya Sai Baba, I have employed the metaphor, a more inclusive one, of Rose-Fire. But this hardly makes any difference. Since Divinity is something that can only be defined and explicated in terms of imagination and poetic perceptions of pure hearts and beautiful souls in prayer, the perpetual Star also becomes the multifoliate rose of heaven. The Rose-Flame descends on the Shirdi soil and after completing the *Avataric* Design it again walks the earth at Puttaparthi.

Professor Gokak has very nicely summed up the question of identity and apparent differences in the modes of the working of two avatars, when he comments:

> Even then, how does it matter if the two prophetic roles are regarded as different from each other. It is the same Divine — Existence — Consciousness — Bliss that works in the other Great ones as well. In a special sense, through certain common characteristics, the same Divinity works in a more intimate way through Shirdi and Sathya Sai manifestations. I once saw Sathya Sai Baba looking at a large portrait of Shirdi Baba, sitting in the famous cross-legged pose, the right leg thrown across the left lap and the left hand on the right foot. Sathya Sai looked at it amused for a while and said in Kannada with a smile, moving his head a little, Aha, Enu Jambha! (Aha, what vanity!) He seemed to say, 'You deliberately wear these rugged clothes. You have chosen a dilapidated *masjid* to live in. You live in a village dead to the world. You do this, so that your supreme self-confidence may shine through them all the more and the world be put to greater difficulty to find out that you are the King of Kings.'
>
> (V.K. Gokak, *Sai Baba: Man and Avatar*, pp. 69-70)

Professor Gokak goes on to say:

> These can be regarded as Sathya Sai's comments on himself through perceived identity. They can be regarded as comments on the other role that the same Divinity was acting. A new dimension is added to our understanding of either of them—realising the actual identity and apparent difference.
>
> (V.K. Gokak, *op. cit.*, p. 70)

Shirdi Sai Baba was truly a major incarnation of the Ray Supreme. The very Alpha and Omega of his destined sojourn on earth was mainly for *loka-kalyan* or the benefit of humanity and to bring about spiritual transformation of the hearts of men. He worked ceaselessly to fulfil his mission. The bright lamp of his noble and redemptive task has illuminated the world at large and is serving as a Lighthouse for the entire humankind tossed on the perilous seas of the material world, the world of endless misery and pain. To take man to the glorious and rose-lit pathway towards God is verily the avowed function of an *Avatar*. This perpetual star descended on earth and chose Shirdi as the place for his earthly sojourn under circumstances still shrouded in mystery and comparatively unknown to the world until Sri Sathya Sai Baba in his Divine discourse on September 28, 1990, threw light on the circumstances of his advent. This may sound strange and unique that a world teacher and a major Incarnation should spend full sixty years at a remote and land-locked village, initially hostile to him, and yet take his devotees to Light from darkness, from ignorance to knowledge and from death to immortality—is indeed a wonder of the highest kind. But this is nothing new. We are aware that the life and career of the Great ones are both inscrutable and incomprehensible. Lord Krishna, rated a full incarnation, was born in the prison-house. Jesus Christ was born in a stable. Ramkrishna Paramhansa took his birth in a small cottage at Chandramauli village and still the glory and splendour of these perpetual stars spread worldwide and became a source of light, love and bliss for the entire human race. A dispassionate glance at the life and career convinces the readers about the supreme continence, candour, detachment and humility of the *Avatar*. Possessed of God-like power, universal omniscience, omnipresence and omnipotence Baba preferred to take a modest and humble stance. He always said that he was a humble servant of Allah and that his Guru had always been kind to him and it was only with the grace of his Guru that he could relieve the pain and suffering of his devotees. At the same time, the awareness of his role as an *Avatar* was ever implicit in his statements. It would be fair to narrate the passing way of Baba which was as mysterious as his advent. And this brings us to the point that the descent and the ascent are the same. Haven't we the instance of Jesus Christ rising to heaven after his crucifixion?

Sai Baba blessed the proposal for the construction of a temple at Shirdi nearer the Dharmashala saying: 'Go ahead with the construction of the temple, but refrain from installing the image of Krishna awhile. I would myself like to be there. I love this place immensely and would like to spend my life here.' The foundation of the temple was laid at a simple ceremony by breaking a coconut and the building work started in right earnest and was soon completed. But Baba was taken ill and grew very weak within three days. Baba's last wish conveyed to the devotees was: 'I should be placed in the temple. Baba's body temperature kept on fluctuating for several days and on the 18th October 1918, the Vijayadashmi day, he left his body to go to that celestial city from where he had come. According to his last wish, his *Samadhi* was erected in the same temple. Thus Sai Baba, the *Avatar* of Sri Krishna, found his resting place in the temple of Sri Krishna.

Biographers of Shirdi Baba have recorded a few strange incidents that had taken place at Shirdi two years before his actual *samadhi*. Baba once lost his temper and was in terrible rage. He cast aside his dress and looked all round with bloodshot eyes. A close devotee Bhagoji somehow pacified him and forced him to put on the dress. But two years after on the Vijayadashmi day he cast aside his mortal vestment, the body. A few days before Vijayadashmi, a close devotee, Ram Chandra Patel, who was critically ill, prayed to Baba for his life. Baba assured him that he would recover and be all right. The God of Death, Yama, had brought his *hundi* which Baba had returned. He further said that

Tantya Patil's lot is causing anxiety. He will not survive the coming Vijayadashmi. Baba's prophecy came true. Ramchandra Patel recovered from his illness while Tantya Patil became critically ill. On Vijayadashmi, Baba himself threw aside his mortal coil by taking on the illness of Tantya, all on himself. Thus the perpetual star ascended to the Heaven its perpetual home, promising to come again to shed its lustre on the world. He also declared before his *samadhi* that his *avataric* mission had been completed. The Light was gone, but in a different sense, there was only the Light. Because *Avatars* never die. They come and go according to their own volition or *sankalpa* and are not bound by *karma,* their chief motivation being their infinite compassion and boundless love for mankind. But human beings grieve over the passing away of an *Avatar* on account of their limited and finite consciousness. Thus, the news of Shirdi Baba's *mahasamadhi* spread like wild fire in all directions and people rushed towards Dwarkamai in large numbers. The devotees and even the general public mourned and cried their hearts out in utter desolation. The light had gone out of their lives, as it were! The Star that shone at Shirdi disappeared and the whole landscape, the entire creation became dark.

6

A SYMBOL PERFECTED IN LOVE

If one is asked to say what Sai Baba is all about, the answer would be clear and definitive — Love. A German woman who saw Sai Baba for the first time, felt that he was the embodiment of love. And Professor Varoneshky of the University of Arizona, a noted and renowned specialist in the study of aura surrounding the faces of individuals, was struck with awe and wonder because he had never in his life seen such an aura on the face of any individual in the world. He had the wide experience of studying the halo on the faces of great and eminent men of the present century, men of power, statesmen, scientists, artists, social reformers, saints and sages. But all seemed to him to be just human and mortal. But after seeing the halo on the face of Sri Sathya Sai Baba, he felt the thrill of joy akin to ecstasy and wondered if such an expansive aura can ever surround the face of a mere human being. Professor Varoneshky described this particular aura as white and pink of the colour of love. When *bhajans* were sung in the prayer hall, the white and predominantly pink aura turned golden, the colour of the sun and then into an expansive blue, the boundless energy of creation. And we know that blue colour is also symbolic of love. Professor Varoneshky saw in the eyes of Baba a diamond-like brilliance. Though Varoneshky is a Catholic, he felt convinced that aurawise, Sri Sathya Sai Baba was God, the primal source of love. Indeed Sathya Sai Baba was the very quintessence of Love. Many other devotees of Baba have also had the experience of witnessing the halo surrounding the face of Baba. We have already noticed in the earlier chapter how John Scher, an American devotee, witnessed the pink and bluish halo expanding and spreading all over the sky and the faraway horizons.

Sri Sathya Sai Baba has said:

> I am the embodiment of love and love is my instrument, mine is love that is pure, free, selfless and unconditional.

And further he has said:

> Sai is infinite love. It is this love that pervades and appears in the entire universe around us. This love is seated ever in your hearts. The universe is Sai. You are Sathya Sai. Love is my form, truth is my breath, peace is my food. My life is my message.

Through constant reiteration of this love, he has clearly and transparently demonstrated both by precept and actual practice that he is the living configuration of love that only God can be. He is the kind of love that surpasses in magnitude and intensity the love of one thousand mothers.

Sai Baba has declared explicitly that Love is God.

It is love that transfigures and transubstantiates everything and binds all into one volume.

Sai Baba has made some extremely precious and beautiful and memorable observations that are truly reminiscent of the teachings of Jesus Christ and offer concrete and tangible suggestions for mankind to live by. For instance, he says:

> God is the source of all love. Love God, love the world as the vesture of God, no more, no less. Through love you can merge in the ocean of love. Love cures pettiness, hate and grief. Love loosens bonds. It saves man from the torments of birth and death. Love binds all hearts into a soft, silken symphony. Seen through the eyes of love, all beings are beautiful, all deeds are dedicated, all thoughts are innocent, the world is one vast kin.
>
> (Sathya Sai Baba)

And here is another practical and easy way to work for the expansion of this universal love to attain the bliss of attaining God:

> Love for all should spontaneously flow from your heart and sweeten all your words. The best spiritual discipline that can

> help man is love. Foster the tiny seed of love that clings to *me* and *mine*. Let it sprout into love for the group around you and grow into love for all mankind, and spread out its branches over animals, birds, and those that creep and crawl and let the love enfold all things and beings in all the world. Proceed from less love to more love, narrow love to expanded love.
>
> (Sathya Sai Baba)

And furthermore, the practice of expanding the love rhythmically to embrace all and every sentient thing and the recognition of sparks of the same divinity is the end of all spiritual exploration. Baba says:

> When you know that you are but a spark of the divine and that all else are the same divine spark, you look upon all with reverence and true love. Your heart is filled with supreme joy and the canker of egotism is rendered ineffective. Man is seeking joy in far-off places, in quiet spots, not knowing that the spring of joy is in the heart, the heaven of peace is in himself. Love is God; God is the embodiment of perfect love. So he can be known, reached and won only through love. You can see the Moon only with the moonlight.
>
> (Sathya Sai Baba)

Such facets of the divine diamond can be seen and realized through intensive study of all that Baba has said in his discourses and *vahinis*. But the important and crucial question is the apprehension and true understanding of the secret of Baba's extreme love and its redeeming, transcendental power. That is to say, divine love and its eternal radiance and transforming power can only be experienced because as Professor Gokak, the renowned Indian English poet, has said in images of poetry,

> ...But divine love
> is the naked majesty of midnight stars
> It is an infinite and luminous downpour
> That fills all your being
> To the very cells of the body...
> Divine love descends on you
> As from the Milky way

And more and more, the more open you are.
It upholds your sail on the ocean of being
And is the chart(er) of uncharted seas
Human love is the fire of the body
That created man in the image of man.
It is the sallying out of the self to self.
But divine love is the light of the heaven
That recreates man in the image of God.

(V.K. Gokak, *op. cit.*, p. 77)

Sri Sathya Sai Baba has declared that his love flows to everyone, to every sentient thing of the universe. In fact, it is this love that sustains the universe. He says, 'If you take one step towards me, I shall take a hundred steps towards you. If you shed one tear, I will wipe a hundred tears.' His love is selfless and without any condition. 'Love is my very nature,' he says. The greatest attribute of selfless divine love is that it is not bound by the fetters of attachment or craving for any return. It is universal as well as impersonal. In the words of Professor Gokak, 'Baba's love floods the vast spaces of the soul. Although it is marked by supreme detachment, it irrigates the arid heart that it may burst into bloom. It is beautiful itself.' Further, Professor Gokak says:

> At an informal meeting, one of the group asked Baba, 'Swamiji, what is the secret of the` cure that many afflicted persons experience in your presence?' Baba said simply and instantly: 'It is my experience that I am one with every sentient thing, every human being. My love flows out to everyone, for I see everyone as myself. If a person reciprocates my love from the depth and purity of his heart, my love and his meet in unison and he is cured of his affliction. Where there is no reciprocation, there is no cure...' Baba's love knows no frontiers. It overflows all boundaries. Like the universal sun it shines on all, whether they be sun-worshippers or owls.

(V.K. Gokak, *op. cit.*, p. 76)

Sai Baba as the single flame and still centre holding the universe in his palm is the fountain of love, pure love. He is indeed a symbol perfected in love. God who is *Sat-chit-ananda,* Being-Awareness-Bliss, can also be fairly described as a symbol perfected in love. Human love is generally fragmentary just as the finite human consciousness itself. 'Who, if I cried, would hear me among the angelic orders?' That was the dilemma before Rainer Maria Rilke, the modern German poet. Torn up and disconsolate at witnessing the great conflagration during the second world war and assailed by thousand and one doubts and distractions he mused over the human condition and had a true vision of the essential human frailty and human lot. He felt as never before that human consciousness is finite and fragmented in the extreme. But there is another kind of consciousness that is undivided and complete. Rilke saw a series of visions at Scholos Duino. Plagued and tormented by the insufficiency of the human condition, the poet set out to capture that elusive and beautiful vision of supreme felicity as represented by the angels, the lovers and all those who have gone to the world of the dead. Similarly, human love is broken, transitory and fragmented, and the central thrust of the pilgrim soul is to aspire for divine love as also for the final merger with the Eternal Absolute, *Sat-chit-ananda.* Sai Baba in some of his letters and poems, addressed to the beloved students of Sri Sathya Sai College of Arts and Sciences, has urged them to move into another intensity and merge themselves into Him. He says in one such poem:

> Live...live...live in perfect accordance
> with My laws, and wonders will ensue.
> ....
> Let old memories well up in you
> From my subconscious in you...
> Old patterns...
> Old forgotten patterns and thoughts.
> Now plunge them into the Ocean of Light
> Burn them from the Consciousness
> So that you may be
> True emblems of my Being.
> Right now visualise my burning Flame
> Rising higher and higher
> As it burns through you...

It is a flame that is cooling
Cleansing and healing;
That soothes the hidden sorrow...
And leaves you calm and quiet.
....
Test in my Love
Let all that you have been through
In your many lives up to this day,
Melt away in my redeeming Light.
Children of My Being
Dissolve your sorrows and fears in me.
Let me efface all your *Karma*
Come back into my Consciousness, which is your own true consciousness
Let your petty human consciousness fade away, right now,
When you come to me, who am your inner self.
You are My own radiant Glorious Self
No longer separate from Me
Melt with Me, merge with Me...
Become Me.

(B.N. Narsimhamurthi (ed.), *Prema Dhaara*, p. 11)

It is great poetry as it represents the true voice of feeling and the depth of highest kind of ardour and love which are the hall-marks of the Divine. As a Professor of English literature, this author feels frankly and candidly that it nearly transcends all existing monuments of devotional poetry that he has known. In the greatest of devotional poets, from Dante downwards to Milton, Donne, Herbert and Vaughan...to Mira, Tulsidas, Hopkins to T.S. Eliot, the motivating force has been the prayer and the supplication of the meditating and the praying mind to voice the spiritual aspirations of the poet in apt and adequate metaphors of poetry. Most of such great poetry has either been devotional or else visionary, tenuous or abstract. But here is another kind of poetry, not penned by the aspirant praying for the one barely prayable prayer for the one Annunciation, divine grace and mercy from that Ocean of Mercy. It is the blessing and grace of the Divine exhorting the devotees to merge with Him and become Him. In this sense, it is the fullest gift of grace and love that mankind can ever hope to realize. This is a burning example of what Divine Love can be and how it can confer salvation on the spiritual aspirant. In another beautiful prose passage, Sri Sathya Sai Baba explains and points out the plenitude of Divine Love:

> My dears,
>
> Sai is Love. He is compassion and kindness itself. He is ever dwelling in the hearts of you all. To trust him means freedom from all anxiety, fear and doubts. He is you, all-in pall. When you have a Lord of the Universe to depend upon why should you be afraid or anxious about anything? His great assurance should always sustain you...The Almighty Lord of the world is seated in your heart, is the sole doer. You are mere puppets. Let him make you dance as he wills. Yours is not to question 'Why?' Difficulties and worries are not due to outside causes. They are due to a mind not surrendered unto God.
>
> With love and blessings,
>
> Baba

In another beautiful and memorable poem, Baba voices his great love for the students and uses resilient and functional imagery of a rare sort. The sense of complete oneness or unity of the human and divine could not have been better expressed than in the following lines:

> The bird with you, the wings with Me;
> The foot with you, the way with Me;
> The eye with you, the form with Me;
> The thing with you, the dream with Me;
> The world with you, the heaven with Me;
> So are we free, so are we bound;
> So we begin and so we end;
> You in Me and I in you.

(Baba, *Prema Dhaara*)

Sai Baba, as we have seen, is the repository of love, the perennial comforter of bruised and torn hearts. He knows the agitation of every mind. One may wonder, who, then, devised the torment, Love? No, the torment is the fruit and consequence of the wrong done to others, to oneself and to one's innate nature which yearns for love. But for many, love is an unfamiliar name. So, mankind is prone to wear the Nessus shirt or the shirt of flame because he misses the meaning of love which alone can redeem him from torment and suffering and make him conscious of his divine heritage and take him on to the Godward path and make him realize the state of eternal bliss, Existence, Consciousness and Bliss. Baba points out the secret of attaining God realization through *sadhana* which is an exercise in the expansion of love for all: Only through Love of God can you attain such bliss (bliss of which is inexhaustible), and develop it into full fruition...It is only divine love which is equal to Him. Foster such devotion in your hearts. Most of you have not understood the principle that Swami embodies, nor can you comprehend. Understand Sai's love. You cannot trace any selfishness in any corner of Sai. Whatever he does, it is for your sake. There is nothing in this world which Sai needs...

> Camphor is white as also the celestial cow,
> Stars are white as also the wings of a swan,
> And so is the sweet smile of Beautiful Sai,
> Sweeter than sweet juice of sugarcane or
> even the wine, is the Love of Sai.

The Love of Sai is more soothing and comforting than the sight of a beautiful flower or the sweet smile of an innocent child:

> Sai's word can confer all joy, happiness
> And prosperity on the world
> Sai's look can shower the delight of the
> rain of the parijaatha flower
> Sai's Hand can confer the comfort of
> a loving mother's hand.
> This alone is your joy and welfare—
> The conferer of Love.

(*Prema Dhaara,* p. 69)

Since Sai Love is infinite and embraces in its orbit the entire universe, it is flowing to us now and forever. Sai Baba is our divine parent, so loving and so caring. Many sincere devotees have experienced the comfort and relief coming from him in moments of crisis. One remembers in this context the famous poem of G.M. Hopkins where he voices his tone of desperation and anguish at not receiving the divine comfort. He voices his agony in his characteristic style:

> No worst, there is none, pitched past pitch of grief,
> More pangs will, schooled at at forepangs, wider wring,
> Comforter, where, where is your comforting,
> Mary, mother of us, where is your relief?
>
> (G.M. Hopkins, *No Worst, There is None*)

Hopkins voices his sense of anguish and desolation. But in Sai Baba there is the loving and caring parent who is always beside his children. Baba has said:

> I am always with you, behind you, beside you, in front of you, in your very heart.
>
> (Sathya Sai Baba)

And furthermore, he says:

> You shed one tear and I will wipe a hundred from your eyes.
>
> (Sathya Sai Baba)

He also assures mankind that God is ever ready to help man in calamitous time and clime:

> God is the nearest, the dearest, the most loving, the most eager companion for man.
>
> (Sathya Sai Baba)

Not only this, Sai love is so powerful, expansive and intense that guards and protects all those who reciprocate his love and surrender to him. This love is, in nature, both protective and redemptive. In another beautiful poem, Sai Baba gives positive assurance to his beloved children that he is always with them:

> Dear, dear loved one
> You ask:
> How will you know when I am near you?
> When on a sultry night
> Everything is hot and still
> The first cool breeze
> Brushes your cheeks
> I am caressing you
> Think of Me.

When the pangs of hunger are satisfied
And loneliness is pierced by happiness
Think of Me.
When I sprinkle your face with rain
And wash the earth, the dry brown leaves
The first smell of clear rain
I am cleansing you.
Think of Me.

....

When pain dissolves
And fear disappears
Think of Me.
While steadfast eyes are horrified
By the cruelties of life
The first glance of the silent setting sun
I am comforting you
Think of Me.
Then you ask:
How will you know when you are near me?

....

When pain becomes unbearable
You smile
And you love Me.
When I take from you
Your most cherished possession
On the first loss of your sight
Darkness envelops you
And you love Me...

For everything you see, hear, smell, taste or touch belongs to me. So how can you give to me what I already am but your love? And that I gave to you before time began as your sole possession. When you return it to me, then you will know you are truly mine and I will dissolve your sorrow and happiness into me. That....being me, I will place you in Bliss forever for I love you and think of you constantly.

From your most loving Father.
(*Prema Dhaara,* pp. 7-8)

Sai Baba being both the Divine father and mother, the creator and the preserver he is always with us sustaining our love for him. And we love him because he first loved us.

Thus, we come to the inevitable conclusion that Sai love is many a splendoured thing which like a sunbeam gives life and energy to all. And like a rainbow it is compounded of many colours. It has multiplex dimensions and can be fully absorbed and assimilated if one is ready to receive it. Its sure and most remarkable manifestation takes place only when the positive and negative poles of electricity meet in unison. This analogy of the electric current has been given by Sai Baba himself when he explained to Mr. R.K. Karanjia how the miraculous cures, remote-controlled surgical operations, rescue of the devotee from drowning and other such critical situations overtake the devotees. The effect of Sai love is exquisitely comforting and far-reaching and its limit is the sky itself. Baba's love is greater than the sum-total of the love of a thousand mothers. At the same time one cannot understand the magic and alchemy of this love and its boundless transforming power unless one has experienced it oneself. In this context, it may be fair to quote here the statement of Professor V.K. Gokak. When questioned by the representative of Movement Newspaper in America how living with Sai Baba so closely for many a year has affected his own character and being, Professor Gokak said:

> M.N.: I have heard you say that living so close to Baba you sometimes can get 'burned'. To what does it refer?
>
> Gokak: It means that he is all perfection. In that light around him, no iota of untruth can survive. No insincerity can have any place around him. But we are imperfect; that is why we are human. In our dealings with him we will try sometimes to impose that imperfection on him without our knowledge. He is very sorry for us because he knows that we are going to be burned...but if one understands what is happening that it is the impurity that is being burned, then one can understand it all right. Plus, there is Baba's game...While this is happening, his love is still there...It still flows to the person. This is what saves and heals him...You are on the

> top of a volcano...As Baba has been saying 'The nearer and dearer you are, the greater are your chances of getting *burned*.'
>
> (V.K. Gokak, *op. cit.*, pp. 49-50)

Professor Gokak has given a personal testament saying how Sai wrought a miracle, bringing about a sea-change and transformation in his emotional life. A poet that he is, Professor Gokak says that his personality was an adamant rock that prevented the waters from flowing out. His predominantly intellectual make-up, spirit of detachment, restraint, poise and central control of emotions prevented him from giving vent to his feelings. He says that the living contact with Baba took him from the arid desert of impersonality to the vast expanse of emotion. It seemed as though Baba had cut a little of that adamant rock to allow the fertilising waters of love to flow. That is what Baba did for him without his knowing it. At this stage, the present author, who had known Professor Vinayak Krishna Gokak for a number of years, nearly thirty years, can very well testify to the change registered in the personality of the learned professor and an eminent intellectual of the country. Having worked with him at the Indian Institute of Advanced Study, Simla where Professor Gokak was the Director, and again at Prasanthi Nilayam where he was the founder Vice Chancellor of Sri Sathya Sai Institute of Higher Learning, the author had numerous occasions to perceive the soft, tender, warm and affectionate nature of the late Professor. Indeed, the gush of the fountain of love and jets of its energy came out unhindered from the inner spring of his heart.

Another reference and grateful acknowledgement to Baba for bringing about a change in the nature and world-view by the impact of Baba on his personality and character has been made by no less a person than Dr. Samuel Sandweiss. He says in answer to the following question:

> Question: Dr. Sandweiss, you described in your chapter on psychiatry a new element that Sathya Sai Baba has added to your understanding of human nature—that of divine love. Can you tell us a little bit how that's affected your work in the United States?

> Answer: Baba's love touches us at such depth and with such intensity that one can only describe it as omnipresent, unconditional, boundless, divine. It is his greatest gift to us, a gift that transforms the devotee—and I'm sure will transform the world as well. My first experience of this love was so profoundly moving that I saw in it the basic force which supports and sustains us all. Since then I have come to see my life's work as trying to purify my own capacity to love, to express this love with those who come to me for help and to help modern day psychotherapists come to know of this love that heals all illnesses.
>
> ...Perhaps I can begin by describing the impact and meaning of my first experience of Sai love. Throughout my personal and professional life, I had been searching for peace of mind, how I achieve this for myself and help with its achievement by others...Although many patients were brought through crisis and felt better emotionally; there was still uncertainty, worry and unresolved sufferings in their lives. Still unanswered were such basic spiritual questions as 'Who am I in the vastness of this infinite universe? Why am I here? What is the purpose of my life? How shall I lead it?' I could see that Western psychiatry had no answer. Neither I nor my patients had the deep sense of peace and protection in our lives that one would hope to find a closer relationship with a loving, caring God.
>
> (Samuel Sandweiss, *Spirit and the Mind*, p. 125)

This may be considered to be a very revealing, convincing and vital statement of Sai love not only for its impact on the personal level, but also for its therapeutic value. Dr. Sandweiss goes on to describe his feeling of ecstasy and bliss on receiving the shaft of sunlight that Baba's love indubitably is. He says:

> Onc evening after hearing Baba speak to his students I retreated dejected and almost broken. I stood a great distance away from him, many walls and many people separating us. I was in the moment of my greatest pain, attracted by Baba's greatest vitality, love and sheer beauty—yet wanting to retreat...I pictured myself being a penniless outcast...As I stood, steeped in this dark cloud of pain, I looked up to find

> the most precious, tender healing light of love I had ever witnessed. Baba came directly to me, smiling tenderly and playfully—capturing me in the radiant light of sheer bliss which sparkled in his eyes. I was immediately immersed in his great joy—and happy beyond measure...He reached out and gave me a small piece of candy—but the spiritual gift was immeasurable. What an immense revelation to me; his understanding of another being deeper than anything I'd ever realized before. In an instant he showed me he was nearer to me than my very breath, that he actually resided in my heart, and, what's more, he responded to my pain. He had waited for the moment when I would be ready to understand—and accept. In this tender, intimate act of compassion, I saw the glory of his omniscience and omnipresence, the mighty transforming and healing power of his unconditional love. And he wanted nothing in return.
>
> (*Spirit and the Mind*)

The personal experience of Dr. Sandweiss is no longer personal; it is the externalization of the innermost realization in the internal castle of the mind, the awareness of a love that is truly like a boon and a blessing. It fertilizes the groundswell of one's urges and apprehensions to soar highter and still higher and to purify and expand one's love beyond self. Baba has said in his own inimitable way:

> Love. Love alone can bind you to others and to God, who is the embodiment of love. Love knows no fear, no anxiety, no grief. I am love. I shower love.
>
> (Sathya Sai Baba)

Perhaps, it may not be out of place at this point, when the glory, the splendour and the majesty of Sai love, which is mysterious, unique, infinite and unknowable, to relate some of the deeply felt tremors of that love which this author has come to realize during the moments of his calamitous torments and sufferings and how soothing, sweet and comforting can this love be in which one gets fully immersed with the whole soul alive and have a fair glimpse of divine love. The author would share some of the contours and magic of Sai love and for this purpose a narration in the first person may be necessary and desirable for the simple reason that only within the texture of subjective presentation can the immediacy and urgency of an intimate journal be properly communicated to others. Such an account may fairly be described as a personal testament.

I lived a, more or less, lucid, calm and serene existence in my adolescence and early youth. I was noble and idealistic and loved people as loving was my innate and original impulse. I was full of the milk of human kindness. Deeply attached to my family of parents, brothers and sisters, I was ever ready to make the maximum sacrifice for them. An emotional and loving temperament was my greatest acquisition and strength. This was at the source of my kinship with people. Coupled with this, I was endowed with a creative imagination that expressed itself in my creative writings in Hindi short stories, to be more precise, and at a comparatively tender age while I was studying English literature at the Bachelor and Master's level, I had the privilege of being known all over the country in the field of Hindi fiction as a promising young writer. My short stories appeared regularly in prestigious magazines and periodicals of the country and they were taken note of by general readers and critics alike. By the time I graduated with honours in English literature and joined the master's course as graduate student in the same subject, two collections of my short stories had been published. And there was no turning back; the sky seemed to me to be the limit. And then dame Fortune smiled on me and I was awarded a teaching Fellowship of substantial value from an American University and I spent nearly two and one-half years at the university and was awarded the degree of doctor of philosophy in English. My doctoral dissertation on T.S. Eliot's later poetry was highly commended by the examiners...so much so that my major professor said that I was the best student he had ever had. And another German Professor was simply lyrical in my praise. He gave me a testimonial saying that 'Krishna is a poet, not the kind of poet who writes verses. He is a poet who sees the simple in its inexorable complexity and the complex in its tantalizing simplicity. He will be an eye and a voice to his people. Whoever will be kind to Krishna will receive the blessings that come from a noble mind and a beautiful soul. He is an honour to his country and a source of pride for all men.'

I experienced the warmth, love and admiration of all my fellow students, teachers and the President of the University which filled me with ecstasy. I was truly on the crest of the wave. Back in India, I was in for a phase of disaffection and disillusionment. I was baptized in pain and suffering and even the Gods who love honest and sensitive men put me on the wheel of fire. My efforts to get a good position in the universities failed and I felt terribly sad and disconsolate. What was worse, the very base of my life, my family posed many a problem for me. My only daughter, Rashmee, showed symptoms of the terrible disease schizophrenia when she was a teen-aged student in the high school and I knew for the first time how unnerving and tragic the whole situation can be. Life, then, became a blazing inferno, a cauldron of fire where I had to dance in measure like a dancer. My very existence, safety and work were threatened, for there was no knowing what would happen the next day. Rashmee was very unwell. She raged and raved and it became increasingly difficult to contain her or to keep her in the house. I took her to all the major psychiatric clinics and sanatoriums of mental health, but there was absolutely no relief whatsoever, and the tender plant that she was, withered and there was no end to the withering of flowers. It was at this time that I sincerely prayed to some super power to terminate the torment and save the life of my beloved daughter. At that time I was serving as a Visiting Fellow at the All India Institute of Advanced Study, Simla, where Professor V.K. Gokak was the Director. As he knew about my problems, so he sincerely advised me to pray to Sai Baba. It is he who can cure her. 'Look, Professor Sinha, yours is a difficult problem in which none else but God can help. It is a dilemma which I myself had gone through. My daughter, too, had mental weakness. I kept her at home and had to pay the price. I was away to the United Kingdom on a short-term assignment as Visiting Professor at Leeds University. One morning when I was going to the university to continue my lecture on Indo-English Literature, I got that dreadful news through a cable from home. My crazed daughter, poor girl, had jumped down the well in the compound of my house and had thus ended her life. It was a tremendous shock but assuming that work is worship, I proceeded to the university and somehow delivered my lecture with a broken heart. There is nothing one can do but bear the onslaughts of outrageous fortune. The other alternative, though it may sound extremely callous, even heartless, is to put your daughter permanently in a lunatic asylum so that you can live in peace. This is a pragmatic approach and perfectly logical and practical. But I know it is easier said than done. Of course, Sai Baba can cure her by his Grace. Why not take a chance?' Professor Gokak whispered in a sibilant voice.

However, the situation took a turn for the worse. Rashmee suffered yet another setback and lost her balance altogether. I got alarmed and felt that I would lose her in the hilly terrain of Simla with deep ravines and precipices. So I had no option but to resign my post prematurely and rejoin my post at Bihar University, Muzaffarpur. Soon a research student, Miss Shelia Prasad, came to see me and offered me a coloured photograph of Sri Sathya Sai Baba. 'Sir, I am aware of your problem. Please worship Sai Baba. He is an ocean of mercy. He will listen to your prayer, I believe.'

Thus, there was the beginning of the end of my problem. The visiting card of Baba poured in the shrine and fragrant aroma of *vibhuthi* appeared on the pictures as well as on the floor. The whole house smelt of a strange aroma and excitement was high. My ardent desire now was to visit Puttaparthi and to seek the blessings of that God incarnate who walks the earth in human form. But where was the wherewithal, the money to undertake that long trip? But Baba had a different design for me. His calls are strange and unique and when the right time comes, even *Karma* has to be burnt out. Another research student of mine, a lecturer in a women's college, had submitted her doctoral thesis on the poetry of Wallace Stevens, under my direction. I had put Professor Narasimmaiah of Mysore University on the panel of examiners. Although he had given his approval to the thesis, he declined to travel way up north to conduct the *viva-voce* test of the candidate; rather he suggested that the test could be arranged at Mysore itself should the administration of Bihar University agree to it. The Vice Chancellor of my university was pleased to sanction the holding of *viva-voce* test at Mysore. And in the summer of 1973, I proceeded to Mysore along with my wife and daughter. The candidate and her husband also accompanied us so that there was good company. After the *viva-voce* test was completed, we made our maiden journey to Puttaparthi and waited tensely for the *darshan* of Baba. Swami went straight to the women's section in the *darshan* line and picked up my wife and daughter for a personal interview. And Baba asked Rashmee, 'Where's your papa? Call him.'

Words fail to describe that momentous interview which was bound to have a lasting impact on me and initiate me to the world of deathless devotion and ardour without end and love unlimited. Baba took me to an ante room below the stair and looked at me with his eyes brimming with love, 'Ah, what a suffering!' I remember, there was so much of feeling and concern over my lot and that of Rashmee. I instantly broke down and tears gushed forth from my eyes. 'Swami, you know everything. Now I have come to you.' Baba smiled serenely and said, with great assurance in his voice, 'Don't worry. Swami will set right everything. She is mentally weak, but she will gradually improve. Give her the *vibhuthi* in a tumbler of water. She will be all right.' We knelt at the lotus feet and holding the packets of *vibhuthi* emerged out of the interview room to the open field lit up by the rosy beams of the setting sun. I felt comforted and radiantly happy, and said to myself, 'there must be some merit in your life that after so much of suffering and parched landscapes of your life, Baba, like the benevolent God, has sent you rain. His words never fail. Be assured that Rashmee will recover from her ordeal and be whole subsequently. So, cheers!'

I mused: hadn't my cup of suffering been full? And I grieved and grieved and cried in total anguish and ceaseless torment. I wondered if there was some super power in the cosmos that could bring me relief like sunlight on a broken column. And I had waited all these years of crucifixion and baptization in pain for the advent of a ray from the supreme which could open up for me the new vistas and avenues of hope, faith and love. I returned home with a new sense of faith, hope and love. It was now heartening to notice a gradual and certain change in the mental condition of Rashmee. She was calmer than before and took special keenness in reading books about Sai Baba and performing pooja in the shrine and usually getting ecstatic and thrilled whenever she noticed traces of *vibhuthi, kumkum* and turmeric on the photographs. And what is more, she often reported that she had seen Sai Baba in her dreams. She was quiet and fairly composed and her usual tantrums of the previous months were now a thing of the past. Everything seemed to be going on pretty well and I came to realize that I had found a new anchor for my soul, something to live by. A new awareness had dawned upon me—that of faith. Tender bud of faith, hope and love seemed to sprout and both myself and my wife lived in continual enchantment and feeling of security. But Baba had ordained yet another test for us so as to help us perfect our will in his will. During my outings I used to take Rashmee along with me so that she could feel mentally refreshed and see places. In one such outing, a mishap overtook us. I had an official conference at Magadh University, Bodh Gaya. Rashmee was sleeping on the terrace of the bungalow where we were staying. At midnight, she screamed as though she had a nightmare and rushed towards the stair. She took a false step in the waning moonlight and fell supine on the level ground below the open terrace. It was a calamity; she was rushed to the medical college hospital where X-ray was taken; a hairline fracture in the first lumbar was detected, requiring immediate hospitalization and three weeks' complete rest on bed. The orthopaedic surgeon who treated her, expressed his apprehension that her condition was alarming and may ultimately lead to permanent paraplegia. However, we waited and prayed to Sai Baba to redeem the situation and shower his grace on the unfortunate girl. There was nothing else that we could do in the situation. I took a long leave from work and nursed the patient amidst fluctuating moods of hope and despair. After three weeks, the surgeon allowed the patient to go home and use an orthopaedic belt around her waist and take regular walks in the open air. He told me that he was amazed at the improvement in the patient's condition and wondered how it had come about. Very soon we were back to

Muzaffarpur where the doctor of doctors, our beloved Lord Sai Baba, took the entire responsibility of the patient. By virtue of his omnipresence he arranged for profuse supply of sacred ashes. All that we did was to place a piece of paper in front of his photograph in the worship room and he did the rest. *Vibhuthi* gathered in thick cluster inexhaustibly and it was administered with a glass of water at least twenty to thirty times in twenty-four hours. And the result was astonishing. The improvement registered on the patient was phenomenal and X-ray plates now showed complete healing and her movement and gait became nearly normal. It was indeed a miracle of love, the like of which I had never seen before. As a consequence of this, our faith in, and love for Baba deepened and increased a hundredfold. My wife particularly joined the local Sai Samiti and attended *bhajans* and participated in other social service. At her behest weekly *bhajans* were held at our residence in which a large number of devotees were present and the many miracles continued taking place. Large footprints of Swami appeared on the stairs and the entrance routes and exit doors. The fluorescent tubes were aglow on their own and the scent of jasmines floated in the air. On one occasion, a mysterious visitor in the guise of a demented woman came to the prayer hall and after the *bhajan* was over, she went out and faded in the thin air on the street going out of the campus.

Messages also appeared mysteriously in the shrine and in one such message there was a direction penned in green ink to the author to write a book on Swami. All these phenomena were beyond my comprehension, plunging me in a state of enlightened mystification. And finally, I came to the only conclusion that Baba was surely and truly divine...the very embodiment of love. What he had done for Rashmee was something which only the divine parent could do.

Not that Rashmee was completely normal mentally; she still was excessively emotional and flew into rage at the slightest provocation and always wanted to have things her own way; but by and large, life was peaceful and we enjoyed a session of serenity and pinned our faith in Swami's words that she would recover in good time. His love was in action and had fertilized the very ground of her consciousness. She read all the books on Swami with great relish and regarded him as her saviour. She always kept on insisting that she be taken to Puttaparthi for the *darshan* of her saviour.

However, there was yet another reversion in her mental condition in the year 1977, and this time in the hotel room at Bangalore. Rashmee was tired and fatigued on account of the long journey and did not eat and sleep well. As soon as we booked a room at Kapila hotel, she started fretting and fuming unnecessarily and ran out of the room and rushed to the crowded streets. It was difficult to restrain her. I was utterly hopeless and disconsolate and was at my wits' end. It was night time. There was heavy traffic on the streets and I feared if Rashmee could save herself from being crushed by a car or a truck plying on the road. At that time, help came from an unexpected quarter. At once a driver stopped his *tonga* and accosted me. I told him about Rashmee and her present mental condition. He offered to render all possible help. He persuaded Rashmee to sit on the *tonga* and took her to a hospital. I followed him on a scooter. The doctor on emergency duty advised me to take her to the Institute of Mental Health, which was located twenty kilometres away. Again the *tonga* driver offered to accompany us. He left his *tonga* at the hospital and accompanied us in a taxi to the famous Institute. I thanked him very much. Rashmee was asked to wait in the ladies' waiting chamber so that she could be admitted into the Institute on the morrow. The doctor cautioned me to keep strict vigil on the patient so that she might not run out, a possibility that often happened in the case of deranged minds. I made her sleep on an empty bench and waited outside in the verandah. But sleep and fatigue got the better of me and I lapsed into temporary sleep. When I woke up and cast a look I was stunned to find that the bench was empty and Rashmee was not there. I made a frantic search all round the premises and even looked for her in the sprawling verandah and adjoining lawns and even across the street and tree-lined avenues and gardens nearby. But there was no trace of Rashmee anywhere. I reported the matter to the doctor on duty, but he was of no help either. 'Didn't I warn you to keep a vigil on her? Now what can

I do? Please go out and report the matter to the police station. There is one round the corner. Maybe, they will manage to get hold of her. You should have been careful,' the doctor said in a sulky and accusing tone. My heart beat faster and my mind seemed to reel. Tension filled my bloodstream. Many dark and gloomy thoughts crowded my brain. 'Shall I ever see Rashmee again? What chance was there to locate her in the desert wilderness of the metropolis? Swami, I had brought her for your *darshan* and blessings...and she has been lost and that too in a state of schizophrenic attack. But your will will be done. Please have mercy on her and save her from possible disaster.' I thought and voiced my prayers to Swami. I returned to the hotel where Rashmee's mother was anxiously awaiting our arrival. She looked askance at me, but I could not utter a single word. Sensing that I was dazed and in a state of shock, she asked with concern, 'Where is Rashmee? Where have you left her?' I sobbed and sobbed unable to speak a word. But after a while I composed myself and related to her how Rashmee disappeared from the waiting chamber in the Institute when I temporarily lapsed into sleep. She consoled me and said gravely, 'It is not your fault. It's all her *karma* and her fate. But do not worry. For those who have no refuge, there is Swami to take care of them. His love for Rashmee has always been demonstrated and I have no doubt in my mind that he would protect her this time as well from any calamity. Let us go to Whitefield rightaway.' She said in a warm and resonant voice which seemed to ring with firm faith and conviction. When the day dawned and the golden rays of the sun wove patterns of red and vermilion we were on way to Brindavanam, Whitefield with one member less. All our thoughts were now centred on Swami. We reached Brindavanam and waited in the *darshan* line. I scribbled a note hurriedly praying Swami to intervene, and handed over the note to Swami when he came near me. He cast a glance which seemed to caress me as though waves and waves of sympathy rolled over to me at least so it seemed to me. When Swami returned to his bangalow and the *bhajans* started we sat all through the session, thinking only about Rashmee and her sad plight. Time passed. We did not even care to have the morning tea or breakfast and even at lunch we did not feel like taking any food. It was an Ash Wednesday for us. How could we think of taking any nourishment when Rashmee was not with us and she might be hungry, desolate and without protection. She was my daughter lost, the favourite child so near and dear to me and the prospects of her recovery seemed very dim indeed! We could not even summon the courage to get back to the hotel and brood over the consequences of what had happened. Doubts assailed my mind once again. Swami had blessed her and had promised to set right everything. But in spite of improvement in her mental condition for some time, there had been a reversion landing her in a difficult situation when her safety and well being has been threatened. So, we remained at Brindavanam for the whole day and attended the evening *darshan* and prayer. But nothing pleased us and we desperately prayed to Swami to do something and soon. When the shadows of the evening lengthened and dusk spread its inky mantle on the streets, buildings and the facade of the horizons, we reluctantly boarded a city bus and alighted near the Railway Station. Once again, gloomy thoughts gripped our mind and tears trickled down our face. As we moved slowly towards the crowded street near the Kapila hotel, we saw a swarm of people crossing the road. And we recognized a form resembling Rashmee in the melee of the unfamiliar crowd. As she came closer, there was no doubt. It was she—Rashmee, my beloved daughter. Was she the long lost daughter of King Pericles in Shakespeare's *Winter's Tale*. Feeling surged in our hearts and tears of joy welled up in our eyes. I fondly embraced Rashmee. She looked tired and was coughing. 'Where had you been last night and the whole day today?' I asked her in a numb voice.

'I was with Sai Baba,' she said enigmatically.

'O.K. you must be feeling hungry. Let us go to the cafe across the road. We shall have some coffee and talk,' I told her.

Seated in a secluded cabin of the cafe, I ordered some snacks and coffee and felt a deep sense of repose now that the precious and lost member of the family was with us. She looked fairly quiet and composed as though the delirium and the hysteria of the previous night had subsided.

'Now tell me, dear, what happened when you slipped out of that waiting hall?'

Rashmee said something that was truly amazing. She said: 'I ran out of the hall because I had the impression that it was a hospital for mad people. And I was very angry with you because I suspected that you would leave me here alone amidst mad women. I was terrified and ran out. I walked out of the hospital and came on the desolate street. There was no traffic and no one was walking on the street. I found a park adjacent to the road and entered it. I found a bench and slept on it. Early in the morning at day-break I was aroused by the piercing rays of the sun falling on my eyes. I remembered that I had none to look after me, both my mother and father had left me alone and conspired to put me in a hospital for mad women. So I sobbed spasmodically. At that time a *fakir,* wearing a loose gown and a cloth tied to his head, came near me. He asked me tenderly, 'Why are you crying, baby?'

'My parents have left me. I have to go to Whitefield to see Sai Baba. Can you tell me how to go there? Can I get a bus to Whitefield?' I asked him. He thought for a while and said, 'You have not taken any food. You must be feeling hungry. Come with me. I will take you to an eating place and put you on a bus back to the place where your parents are staying. They have not left you; rather they are worried about you.' He bought some groundnuts for me and took me to the bus stand.

I asked, 'Tell me, father, who are you?'

'Have you been to Shirdi? No? Come some time. I am always there,' he whispered.

'But I have to go to see Sai Baba at Whitefield. Which bus will be going there?' I enquired.

'Think that I am Sai Baba. First go to the place where your parents are. They are greatly concerned about you. Then you can go to Whitefield,' he advised me.

Rashmee continued, 'I reached the Railway Station and for the whole day I have been wandering on the street. Papa, I must tell you the *fakir* looked very much like that saint whose picture is in our worship-room at Muzaffarpur.'

'You mean Sai Baba of Shirdi?'

'Yes,' she nodded.

It was a night of rejoicing. Next morning I took the bus to Brindavanam, Whitefield and waited for Swami to come. He came out and moved gracefully. The whole sky was lit up with the purple and pink aura and the sky seemed to become orange. He came straight to me and paused for a while, then he smiled faintly and whispered, 'So you have got her. Are you happy now?' He sailed ahead, leaving me in a state of trance. It was a message of joy, perennial joy. Here was the loving and caring God ever ready to help us in the hours of our need, all-knowing and omnipresent.

His love for Rashmee has again and again been manifested, the positive poles of the electric current meeting the negative one. As years have passed, Rashmee has shown steady progress towards normalcy. But for that temporary reversion at Bangalore, there has been no more disturbance in her mental poise. It may be said that Rashmee's life is full of Sai love and it has taken her out of critical situations. Another instance of Sai love can be related when in 1990 Rashmee had some recurrence of pain in the spine and she was really miserable. Sitting in the *darshan* line at Prasanthi Nilayam, she was awaiting the arrival of Swami. It started raining very heavily. Many devotees thought that it was an ordeal by water. In another sense, it was a downpour of divine love, at least so it proved to be for Rashmee. She was praying to Swami: 'Swami, how can I bear this pain in my back?...I do not want to live in this condition...either cure me of this or take me to yourself for eternal rest...' There was commotion in the line as Swami came to the devotees on a car. Many village maids had thronged the place and as Swami approached, they rushed towards him. Rashmee, who was in the second line, was flung down by the terrible rush of rustic women and fell on the feet of Swami. Swami assisted her to get up by giving her a prop and in the process placed his palm on the affected spot in the first lumbar and spoke to her softly, 'Do not harbour such gloomy thoughts. Life and death are not in your hands. Be happy and full of *ananda* always...Swami is always with you. Remember...' Rashmee felt from that moment onwards that all her pain had vanished and she had regained her physical and mental well being. It has been a miracle of love. From these examples, it becomes apparent that the love of Sai Baba is the greatest boon on earth that one can hope to acquire. It is a transcendental sunbeam that illumines the whole soul of man. Thus, Sai Baba, more than anything else, is a symbol perfected in love.

This love operates continuously and on all levels. It was in the year 1985 that I relinquished my position as University Professor and Chairman, Department of English, University of Bihar after the completion of my term of service and joined the University of North Bengal on a similar assignment. But again, Swami had some definite plan for my future and I was one of the few fortunate ones who were asked to serve at the lotus feet. On the fifteenth of July, 1985, I joined the most coveted and prestigious position as Professor and Chairman, Department of English, Sri Sathya Sai Institute of Higher Learning, a deemed university of which Bhagwan Sri Sathya Sai Baba was the Chancellor and Professor V.K. Gokak, the founder Vice Chancellor. I found the maximum level of satisfaction working at an elite institution where work was akin to prayer and the challenges were exciting. I have had the privilege of working at many universities at home and abroad, but never before did I witness such devotion and discipline, such an atmosphere of peace and tranquillity and such a silken bond of love and affection permeating the campus life. Swami was there to oversee the whole programme and loved to meet the teachers and students with a good deal of frequency, addressing them on spiritual themes and transmitting the electric waves of pure love. The teachers sat on the front verandah in front of the *mandir* in the mornings and evenings and Swami was easily accessible to everyone and he spoke to them whenever he liked to do so. There was always a sense of nearness and intimacy and Swami's invaluable counsel was available for the asking. All seemed to bathe in the effulgence and radiance of divine love. Life was all this and heaven too, and I felt that such singular good fortune of being so near to the Lord of the Universe must have meant great merit in one's so many earlier incarnations. At least I felt so and realized that such a sweetness flowed to me that I was blessed and everything about me was blessed. It was a feeling of oneness and belonging to the whole creation, nature, living objects, the earth and the sky and the entire cosmos.

Time passed although I lived in the sempiternal regions of the timeless. And then the time came when one finds oneself on the threshold of illumination—more illumination, and has the epiphany of a rare kind standing at the frontier of life and death. On the eleventh of January 1987 I was face to face with death and oblivion. I suffered a stroke leading to left-sided monoplegia. I had left my quarters to proceed to the annual sports meet of the university colleges at the Hill View Stadium. It was a very important function and Baba was to inaugurate the function. It was dark in the morning and after a night of disturbed sleep I was moving on the busy street, tense and uneasy. Some kind of fever sang in the mental wires and my head was heavy. When I passed by the gate of the College of Arts and Sciences, I remembered that I had to pick up some important papers from my office. So, I turned around and came to my office in the building. My head seemed to reel for a moment and I somehow steadied myself and went to the toilet to wash my face and sprinkle some water on my head. It was then that I felt a severe numbness in my left limb and fell on the floor. I lay unconscious in that condition for a while; then the instinct for survival made me exercise my will. The first thought that came to my benumbed mind was to send earnest and eager prayers to Swami. 'Swami, you are the absolute sole Lord of Life and Death. I have no lust for prolonging my life except to dedicate it to your service. I have still many promises to keep; so I do not want to sleep for ever, not at any rate in the roomless toilet. I do not fear death and oblivion but I have some promises to keep and to make myself worthy of your love. You are omnipresent. Will you pull me out of this desperate situation?' At this stage, I decided to exercise my will and using my right limbs I crawled slowly up to the lavatory door and unfastened the latch. Now I was on the verandah and could see the entrance gate of the college, the green shrubbery, the red and pink flowers and the vast blue expanse of the sky. The effort was too much for me and my energy was sapped. I reclined on the floor and fainted. My head was spinning like a top, and my nerves were on edge. I do not remember how long did that swoon last, but I was aroused from my slumber by a voice: 'Sir, what's happened? You look so terribly unwell. Can I help you?'

'Do please. It seems I've suffered a stroke. Do please run to the Hill View Stadium and inform my colleagues and my family. But first bring a rickshaw and take me to my quarters. I want to rest,' I muttered in a feeble voice.

The young man disclosed his identity saying that he was an assistant in the college and when he was passing by the college gate, he heard a voice directing him to go to the college. 'Don't worry, I'II soon be back with a rickshaw,' he said. He was very helpful and took me to my quarters. When he left the room, I lapsed into sleep and lost all sense of time and space. When I opened my eyes next I was lying in a cabin in the Sathya Sai hospital under the shadow of an oxygen mask and saline water was being injected through my veins. I saw my wife and daughter, both standing near my bed and anxiously looking at me. When I opened my eyes, the doctors came towards me and asked, 'How do you feel now? There is nothing to worry, your B.P. has come down. You will feel much better tomorrow. Now do try to sleep,' the superintendent of the hospital said.

I have a faint recollection of the goings on in the hospital on the first two days. When I was sufficiently stable and my mind was beginning to be alert, I asked my wife all about it. I was told that my condition had gone on deteriorating in the afternoon and the blood pressure was still rising. The attending physicians were all at sea and hardly knew what to do. They suggested that my wife and daughter should rush to the *mandir* and speak to Swami when he came near them in the *darshan* line. Swami came in the evening to the sick room. He looked intently into my eyes for a long time and withdrew quietly. My wife entreated him to have mercy and save her '*sohag*' (marital state). Swami raised his hand as a gesture of benediction but he did not speak a word. However, the visit of Swami proved to be salutary. By night, the blood pressure registered a fall and eventually became normal. The film of haziness before my eyes was dispersed and I was able to see clearly. I could speak fairly audibly. I beckoned my wife to come near me and told her, 'You look so anxious and disconsolate. But there is no need to worry. Swami will take care of me, believe me.' 'Yes, we have been sending our anxious prayers to him day and night,' she whispered.

'I know...I know,' I mumbled.

On the fourth day after the attack, I was feeling reasonably well, although left limbs were immobile and I lay limp on the bed, unable to sit up or stand. A terrible paralysis had overtaken my nerves and there was nothing I could do about it. In the morning of the fifth day a visitor came to my cabin and introduced himself as a male nurse from Canada. He told me that he was of Indian origin and was settled in Canada and that Swami has asked him to attend on you and help you in your daily chores. He sponged my body with a towel, shaved me and helped me change my clothes and took me out on a wheel-chair to the terrace outside where I found plenty of sunshine, fresh air and a sense of openness and happiness. After many a day I had seen the blue expanse of the sky, the teeming vegetation and heard the sweet and soothing melody of the birds. I cast a lingering glance at the domes of the temple and the huge regal building of the university office located at the top of the hill. In short I felt a sense of oneness with the world of nature and experienced a new upsurge of life within me. Mr. Gopal, the compassionate male nurse from Canada, proved to be a very good companion. He was warm and affectionate and what is more, he was a very good devotee of Swami.

He told me 'You are very lucky, brother Sinha. Swami is deeply interested in your welfare and quick recovery. He has given the doctors a piece of his mind and is not very happy with their initial response and reaction to your critical state. But he has now entrusted me with the job of seeing you and keeping company. He has asked the Vice Chancellor and the colleagues and students of your Department to be with you in the nights so as to provide relief to Mrs. Sinha. I want you to do me a favour. When Swami comes to see you next time, do have a word put through on my behalf. This is my only wish to come back to India and serve at the hospital. If Swami is pleased with my service to you, he may call me here. So, do please commend my case. I shall ever be grateful.'

Since I had already developed a soft corner for him in my heart, I assured him that I would do all I could at the right time.

During my illness, all my friends and acquaintances came to see me at the hospital to enquire about my welfare. I was overwhelmed by their fine gesture of affection and their interest in my well being. Sambhavna, my granddaughter who was studying at the Sathya Sai Primary School, could not come as the Lady Principal thought that the child would be greatly upset to see me in my present condition. Sambhavna was a favourite child of Swami. She had a congenital defect in her heart that required open-heart surgery for plugging a hole in the heart. I had prayed to Swami to cure her and he regularly gave her *vibhuthi* and once when she was down with fever, he had taken her to the hospital himself on his car. The principal of the school used to tell me that the child was really fortunate that she had earned the grace of Swami. The Vice Chancellor, Dr. Saraf, was a regular visitor to the hospital to see me and always expressed his confidence that Swami would see to it that I would soon be all right with the blessings of Baba. In fact, everyone in the campus was watching my condition and was feeling gratified that Bhagwan Baba, who was an ocean of infinite mercy and compassion, would not forsake me. And, assuming the seriousness of my stroke with blood pressure touching 220/110 mark, worse could have happened, heart failure or cerebral haemorrhage, but Swami had sent timely help and had taken control of the whole situation.

Now my condition was very much stable and I was more alert and hopeful than ever, and talked intimately with my family members, doctors and visiting friends and students. The only limiting factor was that there was yet no return of power to my paralyzed left hand and leg. But Mr. Gopal took me out on the wheel-chair to the terrace and I spent longer periods sipping tea, reading a book or just talking to Mr. Gopal about life in Canada. He advised me to go in for physiotherapy at a good centre so that the return of power to the affected parts may be hastened. There was no facility for physiotherapy at the Sathya Sai hospital during the eighties, and it did not seem practicable to go over to Bangalore for that exercise. My son, a Reader in Economics at Magadh University, came to see me, but he could not get a longer leave from his university to be able to accompany me to Bangalore. So, it was decided that I should go back home in Bihar and take intensive course in physiotherapy. But before I left, Swami once again sent word that he would be visiting the hospital to bless me. One morning, word went round that Swami's car had arrived and that Swami would soon come up to my cabin. The Superintendent and other doctors waited in my room. Presently, the orange-robed figure of Swami appeared in the room. He came near my bed and cast a caressing and loving glance at me for a few minutes. His eyes met with mine and it seemed to me that beams of love and only love fell on me and I was on the receiving end. There was no immediate effect except the dawning of a feeling of well-being as though my burden of *karma* had been lifted by a divine miracle, the cleansing ray of celestial love. Swami spoke in a firm voice: 'Professor Sinha, I am very happy with you...very very happy! You need not worry. You'll be all right and in good time. You have still to do a lot of my work...'

I was on the crest of waves of joy at that moment and felt not only happy and sublime, but also very proud of myself. And the words of my German professor in the United States echoed in my mind: 'You are so noble and tender and proud...You are a poet and God loves the poets already!' And now I was experiencing that supreme continence of affirmation coming from the mouth of God himself. I was bathed entirely in the white radiance of divine love. And for a moment it seemed to be that one's sufferings and afflictions, even physical undoing and crucifixion are all for the best because they take one several steps closer to God, even force the divine to bring about the wished for transfiguration and consummation and union by love. As suffering alone had been the ground of my beseeching all my life, I was not surprised that God had heard the voice of my calling and had rushed to my rescue and preservation. I remained in a state of dizzy rapture for many days and the tender, loving words of Swami continued to ring in my mind: 'I am very happy with you...very very happy. You have still to do lots of my work...'

On the fixed date of departure, Swami sent word to Mr. Kutumba Rao to arrange a car to take me and my family to Dharmawaram Railway Station and he also expressed his desire to see me at the time of parting just after the morning *darshan* in the field in front of the *mandir*. It was Mr. Gopal who took me on the wheel-chair to the centre of the field. Most of the devotees had departed and the field was comparatively less crowded. Swami walked up to me. He looked at me lovingly and with perfect serenity and love. He waved his right hand and clusters of thin white *vibhuthi* came into his hand. He rubbed the *vibhuthi* gently on my left arm and leg and gave me some to eat. I was unable to control my emotions and looked on tenderly. Words seemed to fail me. I knew that the hour of separation had drawn near. Swami had called me to serve at the university for three years, but even before the termination of that term, sickness had forced me to leave. Now I shall be thousands of miles away from him and would suffer the agony of separation from my divine master. What could I tell him now? Then words rushed to my mouth and I said faintly, 'Swami, what about Sambhavna? Should I leave Sambhavna here at the school? Should I take her back with me?'

'Better take her with you since you will not be here,' Swami said. Then, showing a pen, he asked me, 'Is it yours?' 'Yes, Swami,' I assented. But it was hard for me to understand how he got my pen. Maybe while he was applying *vibhuthi* on my forehead and the left hand, my pen might have fallen down and he had picked that up. But it strikes me as a symbolic act. He had said I still had to do lots of his work and I surmised that continuing with my job at the university was not possible in my present state of health and there was hardly anything else, much less community work or social service...could come under my purview. But my mind was as keen as ever and my intellectual prowess, sensitivity, vision and insight remained as sharp as before—even sharper with the acquisition of mellowed perceptions and transfiguring force of divine love. I could perhaps devote the remaining years of my life in my creative and critical writings and maybe, I could write my memoirs about Swami, the assignment which he had ordained for me way back in 1973 when in a mysterious message appearing in the worship-room he had directed me to write a book on him. Now that he has made me a humble instrument to write not one but three books about him. I think it is the culmination of my modest work, and the trilogy, for whatever it is worth, will be an offering at his lotus feet if not a coronet to adorn the head of the glorious and beautiful Lord.

Here ends my personal testament which may be of some interest to the readers. At least, it gives me immense satisfaction to record my intimate personal experience of Sai love.

As a sequel to this chapter, I am including the ardent and illuminating recognition of the unique Sai love by an old woman and a small child who have come under the spell of Sai love and have received, in the process, the infinite bliss of *being* and *becoming*. The old lady in question is none other than Elsie Cowan, the noble and pure hearted consort of Walter Cowan who had died in Madras and was resurrected by our Lord Sai Baba. The glorious and pious child brimming with love for Sai Baba is none other than Lynn, the Bal Vikas Child of America whose devotion to Sai Baba is not only unique but total and self-effacing, almost reminiscent of the child Saint Teresa who was so much fired by divine love that she wanted to lay down her life for the sake of the Lord, and embrace martyrdom. Elsie Cowan gives sincere and frank gratitude to Sai Baba for giving her husband, Walter Cowan, a new lease of life. Elsie Cowan records:

> We have come back from India, my husband and I, brimful of the most astonishing news that could happen to anyone. It is so fantastic that many may doubt it because hardly any of us realize the great importance and the tremendous power of this great high God who not only walks the earth, but cares for the planes from earth into eternity. He gives us

strength and power. He is compassionate. But most of all, he gives us the protection with his Grace. In time of need, he wraps his Grace round us like a very warm blanket, soft and lovely to soothe us into a state of bliss. Without Him, there would be no one to turn to; no father to ask; and even greater than that, at the very deepest feelings, He makes us strong. There are no tears for the body goes back to the earth...It is a blessing to know that the great Lord takes care of us, places us where we should be placed, or else as in this case, after several hours, he brings one back to life as he did Walter, my husband.

(Elsie Cowan, 'Sai Baba and the Resurrection of Walter Cowan', *Sai Baba and His Message,* ed. S.P. Ruhela, p. 236)

The story of Walter Cowan's resurrection is too well known and hardly needs any further explication. Admittedly, the resurrection of Walter Cowan demonstrates the great power of divine love that even interferes with the law of nature and one's *karma.* Through the experience of the deceased we have known that it was Sai Baba who intervened with justice of the court in the kingdom of Death that Walter should be returned back for he had not yet completed his assigned work for spreading peace and love in the world. We also know that Jesus Christ resurrected Lazarus from the tomb so as to glorify the Holy Ghost. Sai Baba, on his part, brought Radhakrishna back to life even three days after he had cast off his mortal coil and his body had started stinking. Such is the power of divine love that can work out great miracles for the sake of the deserving devotee.

The story of Lynn is endlessly sublime and demonstrates the quality of love in the heart and soul of the fourteen-year old girl who sang *bhajans* and loved Baba with a devotion that speaks volumes about her ardour and self-surrender. She did not value anything more precious than her devotion to Baba. Indeed, it was her devotion to Baba that brought her two younger brothers and parents closer to Baba. She set an example for the world to follow and showed what divine love can do to the tender, soft, silken and milky mansion of a child's heart.

Mary Lynn Radford, her mother, reports:

> It was Lynn, who after seeing our first Baba film at the center, said, 'Mommie, we must have our own meditation center.' She promptly removed all her books from a recessed bookcase in our back hall, and henceforth it was our altar where we meditated, daily.
>
> (Mary Lynn Radford, 'Unity is Divinity', *Transformation of the Heart,* ed. Judy Warner, p. 136)

Mary Lynn Radford goes on to say:

> ...My pride in her devotion was tempered with occasional thoughts that perhaps the zeal was abnormal for a child of her age. Little did I realize that Lynn was being guided tenderly by our Lord and prepared for the culmination of her short life...It was a Thursday afternoon, ten days before Easter, the all important date of the Christian calendar that commemorates the resurrection of Jesus Christ. School had finished for the day. Lynn had gone to the park, and I knew she was heading for the tall pine, her favourite climbing tree. I remember watching her from the kitchen window as she darted off, calling in her sweet voice for our dog Jupiter to follow. Forty-five minutes later, a neighbor came to call me that Lynn had had a fall...As I ran, I heard Lynn call 'Mommie, mommie'. As I reached her side, she knew I was with her. She lay quietly and did not seem to be in pain; thus I had no idea she was so near death. I prayed earnestly as I held her hand, 'Baba, please be with Lynn...' An hour later, in the Catholic hospital nearby, a priest was administering the last rites as she quietly passed on...Numb with grief, I asked Baba for reassurance. The first thought that came was: 'Why, it is Thursday, Baba's day.' Indeed two short hours after Lynn's passing, *bhajans* and prayers at Santa Barbara center were lifting her spirit.
>
> That night I could not sleep. I was tormented by the knowledge that Lynn, stunned by her fall, had perhaps been unable to think of Baba at the time of her passing. The next morning when I went to her room, Baba had already answered my anguish. There on Lynn's desk were her last

words, written just before going to the park. They were a fateful synthesis of the morning and evening prayers:

'O Lord, I rise now from the womb of slumber. Before I plumb again into the daily routine, let me pray most earnestly Thee, Omniscient Self and seek Thy lap, which confers on me restful sleep and blesses me with eternal sleep and everlasting bliss...'

It became clear that Lynn's death was no accident, but like her life, another part of Baba's tapestry. In the days to follow, other part of the pattern would fall into place, revealing to me as I had never experienced it before, that Baba's loving network was indeed the basis of all existence.

The poetry of paradox was again revealed. We usually consider death as a tragic event, yet in this instance, as a dear friend would say, Lynn's life and death were a beautiful solo in Baba's symphony...I would close with our daughter's own words which she wrote on a family camping trip:

'The golden sun climbs up from behind
Around green hill.
All the sky is blue, cold and open.
Sai Baba stands on a single rock,
Smiling with the glory of dawn.
To Baba, who sits on a golden throne;
Surrounded by snowflakes and forthy sea foam,
Come into my heart
And replace them with a blissful song.'

(Mary Lynn Radford, *op. cit.*, p. 140)

Mary Lynn Radford, the mother of the angelic child Lynn, describes what seems to be the beautiful finale of the destiny of the chosen child so dear to God. She describes it in the following words:

Shortly after Lynn's story appeared in *Sanatan Sarathi,* I found myself in a period of depression. Perhaps the sharing of my daughter's story stirred up some residue of grief or perhaps it was simply one of those dry spells that occur from time to time in a devotee's life. Whatever the reason I found myself praying to Baba for a special sign of his love. I did not specify what it should be, I simply asked for his reassurance.

One week later, my prayer was answered in a most dramatic way. I was surprised to see Mr. Vinu Mukunda distinguished devotee of Baba and talented musician, who had actually played his Veena at Lynn's memorial service three years earlier...I listened as Mr. Mukunda revealed that he had just happened to be present when Mr. Kasturi, according to his custom, was asking Baba's permission for publishing the stories slated to appear in the March 1979 issue. Among them was the story of Lynn which I had submitted to him. Then Mr. Kasturi asked Baba about Lynn, and Mr. Mukunda heard Baba say 'She was a beautiful child and she brought joy to all who knew her. Why hold her back? She has finished her *karma*. She is with me.'

(Mary Lynn Radford, *op. cit.*, p. 140)

The story of Lynn is marked with endless sublimity and demonstrates the overwhelming impact of Sai love on all alike, irrespective of caste, creed and colour. As Baba says, there is only one religion, the religion of love and there is only one God and he is omnipresent. We find that transiucent beam of this love has not only shaped the destiny of Lynn, but has released her from the bondage of her *karma*. The high point of Lynn's spiritual journey and consequent merger with Baba lay in her deathless devotion and pure ardour and a lifetime's death in love. She contained in the closest chamber of her heart the deep craving and unique and infinite yearning for merging the very self with that omniscient Self. She pursued right from her angel infancy the radiant light that shone on the universe like the morning sun on the peak of the green hill. Even before going to the park to climb the tree from which she slipped and journeyed from hither to the farther space, her thoughts were centred on Baba and her urge was for total surrender and easeful rest and eternal sleep. It was truly the tapestry of divine love that directed and shaped her and as her mother felt she had been a solo in Baba's symphony. Such instance of love in thought, action and motif is hard to get by, at least for the grown-ups whose consciousness is tainted by the fury and the mire of the human blood and worldly usages. But for the beautiful child Lynn, it was all purity and intensity of love that works out wonders. Lynn was the quintessence of that native purity, intuition and love that makes one plumb the hidden recesses of one's being and inflames the heart with the spark of divine ember...She symbolizes the deep and profound longing for the divine as was the case with St. Teresa and Meera Bai for whom Jesus Christ and Krishna were all in all. Sri Sathya Sai Baba responds always if he finds that the yearning heart is brimful with love. He says:

> At first God stands at a distance watching your efforts. He is like the teacher who stands aside while the student writes the answer to his questions. When you shed your attachment to the material world and turn to doing good and serving others, God comes increasingly near. He is the sun God who stands waiting outside the closed door. He simply waits. But when the master opens the door even a little the sun rushes in at once and drives out the darkness. When you ask God for help he is right beside you with hands held out to help you. All you need is the discrimination to pray to God, and wisdom to remember him.
>
> (Sathya Sai Baba)

It is not surprising, therefore, that Lynn had kept her heart open and ajar for the entrance of the fresh and lovely rays of the sun God. And that may be the reason why, in her beautiful poem, she used the metaphor of the sun to symbolise beauty and splendour of the divine.

Perhaps, it is time that we should end this chapter on this note and by quoting a beautiful poem by the Lord himself, disclosing the mechanism and dynamics of his own redemptive love that is sweet nectar to all. At the same time, divine love, which has no beginning, middle or an end, flows for ever and impregnates the parched soil of our hearts with a new efflorescence of tender shoots of faith, hope and love. Here is the poem in its supreme beauty and glory:

Walk the earth with your heads held high.
Your spirits soaring
Your hearts open to love
And believe in yourself and God within you
Then all will go well.
The earth is a manifestation of My Being
Made out of my life!
Wherever you look, I am there
Wherever you walk, I am there.
Whomsoever you contact, I am that person
I am in each, in all My Splendour.
See me everywhere.
Talk to me and Love me,
Who am in each.

(Sathya Sai Baba, Children of Immortality,
Prema Dhaara, ed. B.N. Narsimha Murthy, p. 9)

7

MANY A GEM OF GOLDEN RAY SERENE

What is of utmost and supreme significance to man is th inward journey or the spiritual exploration to know the ultimat reality. As for the romance hero, the questor in medieva romances, so for each of us there is the basic need and necessit to undertake the spiritual pilgrimage to arrive where we starte and to know the place for the first time, our real home. Sai Bab of Shirdi often spoke about a foolish young man who went t the seaside with a view to dive deep into the unplumbed depth of the ocean and fish out precious pearls therefrom. He waite all night, sitting listlessly at the promontory and looked forwar to the rosy dawnlight when he would dive into the sea and fis out the precious gems. But as he waited tense and expectant fo the dawning of the light that would make the seascape clear an bright, time seemed to have a stop and he felt utterly bored an disconsolate. So, he looked around and set his eyes on the dar facade of the horizon, not aware of the darkness within his hear In the dim light of the fading moonlight, he saw a mound o stones nearby at the sea beach. So, in order to pass his time an by way of a pastime to while away the desultory moments, h picked up a stone and threw it into the waves. The sound o the splash, produced by the fall of the stone in the water, please him no end. And he continued with his game throughout tha humid and sultry summer night. Just before the day-break, th film of mist disappeared and the horizon's mirror tilted and i that beautiful and tranquil atmosphere, the young man looke at the heap of stones nearby and found that the heap of stone was not as high as it was during the night. He had picked u stone after stone and had thrown them into the ocean. Just ther the first rays of the sun fell on the beach and the remaining stones of the mound shone with a strange glimmer and lustre. The young man picked up a stone and looked at it closely. He found that it was a precious gem of golden ray serene. He cursed himself for his rank folly; he had thrown away the entire treasure of pearls into the sea without knowng it. Sai Baba told the devotees who surrounded him every night at Dwarkamai to hear his words of wisdom, that this was the tragedy of the human lot. He presumes to know himself and considers himself to be clever and wise, but he simply deludes himself by running after strange gods. On account of his inordinate lust and desire for material glory he is all the time hankering after precious pearls from the depths of the sea, little knowing that all the treasure, the priceless gems and pearls are all stored within his own heart and consciousness. Thus, in his foolishness, the young man threw away the precious pearls into the sea and had no option but to lament over his lot. Sri Sathya Sai Baba has also emphasized the fact that man runs after material treasures and overlooks the priceless gems that are buried in his own back garden. Howard Murphet makes this point explicit when he says:

> There is the story of a young man who travelled the world seeking a hidden treasure, the pearl beyond price. Finally, he met a wise man who taught him many wonderful things. The important and most astounding thing was that the buried treasure was buried in his garden back home. He had to dig for it himself but the wise man gave him instructions about how to find it. Likewise, Swami has told me, and all others who drink the cup of his wisdom, that the spiritual pearl beyond price is buried in the garden of one's own heart, one's own spiritual heart. It is there that I must dig for it. So the end of the outward journey, bringing me as it did to the feet of the *Avatar,* the Master of all wisdom, was not the end of my journey. I had to set off on another one, perhaps even more difficult, more hazardous. Swami calls this the Inward journey.
>
> (Howard Murphet, *Where the Road Ends,* p. 272)

Sai Baba, being a great world teacher, has given us the

guidelines for this our momentous inward journey. All that we have to do is to follow his directions truthfully and live by them. His chief stress is verily on a quartet of moral values or human values, whatever we may call them. They constitute a symphony and a quartet so that while the music of one is audible, that of the others is also heard. This is also true of Sermon of the Mount delivered by Jesus Christ to his disciples. It is true that the teachings and messages given by the saints, sages and great *Avatars* have strange, unique and universal quality since they are meant both for the individuals and the widest commonalty so that the entire mankind whose spiritual transformation and regeneration is at the centre of their mission, may benefit by them. Love, Truth, Righteousness, Peace and Non-violence are the five gems that Sai Baba has underlined as the gems of golden ray serene which constitute the central kernel of his teaching and the chief burden of his *avataric* mission. Sai Baba like Jesus Christ is the very embodiment of Love. In the following part of the chapter, it may be fair to describe the full implication of the concepts of Truth, *Dharma, Prema, Santhi* and non-violence and how can they take us on to the inward journey reaching the still centre. At the same time, these five attributes prescribed by Baba are not merely abstract or symbolic virtues. For one thing, they are remarkably precise and concrete and can form the cornerstone of man's spiritual quest. These are composite values falling into a beautiful pattern. They are closely interrelated, one with the other. That is to say, the practice of one of these values leads to the practice of the other. However, the stress on the five human values is not altogether new or original. As we know, these are the gems that we find in all religions of the world and in the annals of perennial philosophy. Since these are the eternal verities which the human race must live by, they have to be constantly restated and reiterated from time to time. Krishna gave a concrete shape to these eternal verities in the song celestial, the concentrated essence of the Vedas and Upanishads and Christ reframed them in his own idiom and transmitted them to crowds through parables. Sai Baba also uses parables and analogies in order to drive home the meaning of his sayings. When the words are clothed in the vesture of thought and feeling, they seem to go straight into the heart and have a profound effect on the listeners. Baba often plays on words and shows his complete mastery of the norms of language. Thus, most of his sayings take on the quality of memorable speech and cannot be easily forgotten.

The five gems which matter most to mankind are *Sathya, Dharma, Prema, Santhi* and *Ahimsa.* If one imbibes these priceless virtues in one's character, he perfects himself in the will of God Almighty, and earns the grace of the Lord for further union and deeper communion with him. These virtues can be acquired through the difficult and arduous process of *sadhana,* a spiritual exercise costing not less than everything. These are the ideals that make man grow into the image of God himself. The acquisition of these priceless gems is a matter of sustained and ceaseless spiritual exploration. The practice on the spiritual plane involves confidence within oneself. Without this self-confidence one can get nowhere. Without self-confidence one is tossed on the stormy seas of confusion and doubt. The first step on the ladder of spiritual ascent, of course, is the confidence in the self, the inner self or *atma* which is the divinity within. As Baba says,

> The first thing you have to do is to develop confidence in yourself. It is people who have no confidence in their own self who begin to wander about and to waver and take to various different paths.
>
> (*Sathya Sai Speaks,* 9, p. 184)

The aspirant must have faith in himself which means faith in the divine. He must chart out his course in the spiritual voyage undeterred by doubt and confusion. Baba has advised people to have full faith in their inner vision because as Baba has pointed out:

> Self-confidence is the basis of faith in God also. People who do not know who they are and have no confidence in their own strength and power assert that there is no God. But how can they declare that the God in whom you believe and who exists for you does not exist?
>
> (*Sathya Sai Speaks,* 9, p. 88)

Truly, self-confidence is the first requisite for the seeker and is the precious gem beyond price; it arises from the *atma,* the inner reality and is of divine origin. The second important step in the ladder of spiritual destination is what is termed as discipline. Sathya Sai Baba lays great stress on practising the right discipline. Discipline is essential for attaining self-realization and is the starting point for all spiritual endeavour. As Baba has rightly declared:

> The real you is the *atma.* This can be learned only by constant meditation, by moving in good company, by listening to the talk of realized men, by following some prescribed form of discipline. That is why I lay so much emphasis on discipline.
>
> (*Sathya Sai Speaks,* 4, p. 159)

And Baba has said the last word on the quality of a disciplined mind and heart in quest of God:

> Discipline comes to the rescue during crisis when the world flows towards you as a dark flood of hate or derision, or when those in whom you have put your trust shun contact and shy away. Without discipline, the mind of man is turned into a wild elephant in a rut. You have to catch it young and train so that its strength and skill can be useful to man and harmless to life around.
>
> (*Sathya Sai Speaks,* 7, p. 418)

Amongst the five gems of golden ray serene, *Sathya* (Truth) comes in the first place and tops the list. *Sathya* is also the name of Baba. It means the unchanging, eternal Absolute which is the chief adjunct of God.

Truth may be described as a pole star that guides our journey through life in the darkest night. Truth is the prime mover since it is the very nature of the divine. It is truly the base and foundation of our *atma.* Truth manifests in action as *dharma* (right action), in our being as love and purity of heart. According to Baba, the search for Truth is the avowed duty and destination of man. Thus Truth is the gem of infinite beauty and splendour, the brilliance of which illumines our existence and saves us from indulging in falsehood. Sathya Sai Baba points out:

> The chief duty of man is investigation into Truth. Truth can be won only through dedication and devotion and they are dependent on the grace of God which is showered on hearts saturated with love.
>
> (*Sathya Sai Speaks*, 6, p. 1)

The unique distinction of man in the entire creation lies in the fact that amongst all creatures in the phenomenal world, it is only he who is bestowed the powers of intelligence and discrimination. It is central to the basic nature of man to seek love and truth, for these are springs of *atmic* origin. We all have come from God, our original home, and it is our duty to return to him.

Thus, the search for truth is basic to human nature and is the sure and reliable pathway that leads us to the supreme since God is truth and when we tread confidently on this path, we are sure to feel at one with God. That is precisely why Truth has been placed at the top of the five moral virtues recommended by Sri Sathya Sai Baba. Baba has very nicely summed up the cardinal importance of Truth as an eminently desirable virtue:

> There is in everyone a spark of truth; none can live without that spark. There is in everyone a flame of love, life becomes a dark void without it. That spark, that flame is God, for he is the source of all truth and all love. He seeks to know the reality because his very nature is derived from God, who is truth. He seeks love, to give it and share it, for his nature is of God and God is love.
>
> (*Sathya Sai Speaks*, 1, pp. 78-79)

After Truth, the next most important gem of moral and human values has to do with *Dharma* or right action. Sometimes, the full meaning and implication of this term is grossly misinterpreted and even missed. It is generally believed that *dharma* means adherence to some religious creed or doctrine and has a predominantly moralistic and ethical content. But it is not fair to take such a limited and restricted view of *dharma*. *Dharma* is an all-embracing term and has a number of connotations. It does certainly have its basis in what we may call moral or religious obligation. But, broadly speaking, *dharma* is the spiritual obligation, attendant on one's responsibility to self, to others and to God and it entails introspection and self-discipline based on the knowledge of one's inner divinity. That is to say, that a person who is not conscious of his inner divinity and is not concerned with his spiritual obligation to self, to others and to God, cannot perform his duty or *dharma* in the true sense of the term.

However, the most puzzling question is to determine how does one perform one's *dharma* or spiritual obligation in action? *Dharma* is something that depends on certain specifics of time and circumstances. According to Sathya Sai Baba there are unchangeable constants which must be adhered to, always and at all times. Baba lists them:

> And what is *dharma*? Practising what you preach, doing the way it has to be done, keeping the precept and practice in line. Earn virtuously, yearn piously, live in the fear of God, live for reaching God: that is *dharma*.
>
> (*Sathya Sai Speaks*, 4, p. 239)

These, then, are the basic, universal laws which are at the core of all religions. They are the golden rules enumerated by Jesus Christ in his Commandments as well as in the Sermon on the Mount. One must strictly observe the golden rule contained in the saying: 'Do unto others as you would have them do unto you.' In a nutshell, Baba has summarised the basics for the observance of the *dharmic* way of life:

> What exactly is your duty? Let me summarize it for you. First, tend your parents with love and reverence and gratitude. Second, speak the truth and act virtuously. Third, when you have a few moments to spare, repeat the name of the Lord with the form in your mind. Fourth, never indulge in talking ill of others or try to speak ill of others or discover faults in others. And finally, do not cause pain to others in any form.
>
> (*Sathya Sai Speaks*, 4, pp. 348-49)

These five injunctions constitute the recipe of a virtuous life dedicated to *dharma* and can offer mankind the mode of salvation. At the same time, these injunctions are not hard to follow for each of us. Nor do they require any *sadhana, mantra* or *tantra.* All one has to do is to chart out one's course in the perilous ocean of *samsara,* keeping always in mind the awareness of one's spiritual obligation. To tend one's parents with love, affection and reverence is just the repayment of one's debt and homage to those earthly people who have given us birth. Similarly, remembering God in one's spare moments is the spiritual obligation and duty of the pilgrim soul towards the heavenly father. And one should always be loving and considerate to one's fellow beings as all are brothers and sisters, emanating from the same divine essence. So, these are the gems of golden ray serene that shine in their intrinsic glory and resplendence.

Sathya Sai Baba has said that his life is his message. He has declared that he is *dharmaswarup,* the very embodiment of righteousness. Although he is not circumscribed by the concept of duty and reason, he is doing his *karma* out of his own volition so as to set an example for mankind and to provide joy to others. His advent has been for *loka kalyan,* and he has founded many educational institutions including schools and colleges as well as hospitals, all for the welfare of the people. Even without having any *karmic* necessity or compulsion, he is devoting every moment of his life for the sake of his devotees, fostering them, instructing them in pious and virtuous living, counselling them and curing them of dreadful and terminal diseases. If one spends a day at the Nilayam, one finds that Baba's day is crowded with activities right from the dawn to midnight only for the benefit of his devotees who are ever so near and dear to him.

Though Love figures in the third place and is third in order amongst the priceless gems offered by Swami, it is the apex and crown of all, since love is the very basis of creation. Indeed love is the primal energy that manifests itself in the creation of whole cosmos, the earth and the sky, the rivers and the oceans, mountains and deserts, the birds and beasts, man and all sentient things. As Baba has very nicely said,

The basis for the entire world is *prema* (Divine love) of the

> Lord. Even if one is able to get by heart the essence of all the Vedas (sacred teachings) and is able to compose poetry in a very attractive manner, if that person does not have a purified heart, he is a useless person. What other greater truth can I communicate to you?
>
> (*Summer Roses on the Blue Mountains*, p. 9)

Thus, love is the central jewel in the well-wrought urn of Sai teachings, the greatest and most precious acquisition of mankind which transforms man into the image of God.

Love is something that has to be cultivated with care. Just as we require the proper fertile soil for the growing of flowers and their blossoming, similarly to grow love into proper, luxuriant bloom, we require to weed out the weeds of attachment and greed and selfishness from our hearts.

Once we realize that love is many a splendoured thing and represents the principle of unity with the eternal Absolute, we begin to work for the expansion of our love beyond the self to include parents, friends and the entire humanity. Since there is no limit to the attributes of God, our love for God is, in reality, becomes all absorbing, annexing all creatures of the created world. The secret dawns upon us that the universe is the image of the divine and expresses the tapestry of God, we begin to see God in all and begin to identify ourselves with everyone. Their joys and sorrows become our joys and sorrows and there is no longer any sense of separation or alienation. Through the alchemy of love we reach our true destination and experience the bliss of oneness with the divine essence. Baba rightly directs us to extend our love for further union and deeper communion with him.

> Love is God, God is love. Where there is love, there God is certainly evident. Love more and more people. Love them more and more intensely. Transform this love into service, transform the service into worship. This is the highest *sadhana*.
>
> (*Sathya Sai Speaks*, 4, p. 309)

It is apparent that all the five moral virtues and human values advocated by Baba are related, one with the other, and their practice involves spiritual exercise of a very high order. As Baba has stated,

> If we really want to experience *Prema* we will have to understand what peace or shanti means. If we want to follow the path of peace we will have to accept the path of *dharma.* If we want to follow the path of *dharma,* we will have to accept the path of truth.
>
> (*Summer Showers,* p. 60)

It is mainly through the expansion of love beyond self that one can reach beyond one's worlds and grasp the importance of universal values. All the great visions of humanity germinate through a heart full of love. If we wish to know and experience God, who is Being, Awareness and Bliss, we must love all the creatures and the creation which are the handiwork of God. When we experience the source of love within, we view the world with glasses of love. Thus, love is the roof and the crown of all values. Sri Sathya Sai Baba emphasizes the supreme value of love as a priceless gem, our greatest acquisition and possession that leads us to our goal. Baba's prescription to us is to follow this way of love in our daily life. He teaches:

> Start the day with love
> Spend the day with love
> Fill the day with love
> End the day with love
> That is the way to God.
>
> (*Sathya Sai Speaks,* 8, p. 73)

And Baba communicates to us the pearl of wisdom when he says:

> I must tell you of the paramount importance of love. Love is God, live in love. God is the embodiment of perfect love. He can be known and realized, reached and won, only through love. You can see the moon only with the help of moonlight. You can see God only through the rays of love.
>
> (*Sathya Sai Speaks,* 8, pp. 181-82)

Peace and Non-violence are the remaining two gems of golden ray serene which are eminently desirable for mankind. Jonathan Roof in his beautiful work, *Pathway to God,* has characterized Peace as the sign of God's creation working in harmony. Peace is like a river flowing from the mountain to the sea along its bank always maintaining its equilibrium with the shore. Everything in the cosmos follows a definite pattern reconciled in the drift of the stars. Thus the creation is preserved and maintained by perfect harmony and balance. Similarly, peace for the spiritual aspirant is a state of spiritual equanimity based on the understanding of his spiritual obligation or duty. When we have a clear perception of the divinity working in the nature and cosmos, we tend to live in consonance with the divine norms and recognize the hand of divinity in everything.

And when one lives a virtuous life one is at peace with oneself. As Sathya Sai Baba says,

> When man thinks, speaks and acts along virtuous lines, his conscience will be clean and he will have inner peace. Knowledge is power it is said, but virtue is peace.
>
> (*Sathya Sai Speaks,* 10, p. 267)

To live in a state of perfect peace and serenity, one has to keep one's senses under control, do away with unreasonable desires and longings. When one has unreasonable expectations, one feels ruffled and upset by failures and disappointments. So, a mind in peace follows the path of the golden mean, thinks, lives and acts wisely and virtuously, leaving the fruit of his action on God. When desires are burnt away through discipline and *sadhana* what remains is the purity of consciousness and the realization of the inner divinity within. As Baba has said:

> There is no mind as such. The mind is a web of desires. Peace of mind is no desires, and in that state there is no mind. Mind is destroyed, so to speak. Peace of mind means purity, complete purity of consciousness.
>
> (*Conversations,* p. 44)

Jonathan Roof has rightly pointed out that:

> *Atmic* peace is our true nature, it is acquired when we look within. If we are concerned only with outward circumstances, the jumble of daily events we will be unable to experience peace. Ignorance of our divine origin causes us to be elated

> or dejected at the changing course of events. Our true nature is selfless love and joyful peace, unbounded by time or circumstance. It manifests when it is allowed to shine through the clouds of illusion.
>
> (*Pathways to God*, p. 182)

The possibility of attaining inner peace or peace that passeth understanding is, after all, not very difficult to achieve. All that one requires for it is to realize that peace is our essential nature, but it is hidden by the clouds of attachment, and the darkness of anger, and selfishness. But if we become aware of our inner divinity and move towards the still centre of our being, the divine self or the *atma* would radiate peace. In the words of Sathya Sai Baba:

> Once you enter the depths of the sea, it is all calm. Agitation, noise, confusion — all are on the outer layers. So also in the innermost recesses of the heart, there is a reservoir of *santhi* (peace) where you must take refuge.
>
> (*Sathya Sai Speaks*, 1, p. 172)

As in the case of the other moral virtues, peace also requires constant spiritual practice for its attainment. Practice helps us to perceive the vision of unity and to see God in everything and everyone. When we see the painful consequences of desires for fleeting pleasures and material acquisitions, we learn to search for more lasting values. Then we turn towards God and attain the peace and the joy that is derived from knowing God. Sathya Sai Baba has said that one has to work for attaining the priceless gem of peace through continual effort and self-sacrifice:

> Our thoughts of God and intense longing for him bring peace. As worldly thoughts diminish, thoughts of God increase. Normally the mind desires these things all the time. As the desires are cut one by one, the peace becomes stronger...when there are Godly thoughts, there is peace of mind. Swami cannot give peace of mind; one has to work for it.
>
> (*Conversations*, p. 22)

However, the mind is like a monkey not to be easily

restrained or stilled. To keep the monkey mind on the leash, the best thing is to repose our faith in God and cling our thoughts to God and God alone. As Eliot says:

We shall be still, and still moving
For further union and deeper communion.

If the mind centres on God, the experience of perfect peace will inevitably follow and peace, thus gained, will be our priceless possession. The attainment of inner peace in the mind of man has a far-reaching consequence. Baba has put it very nicely when he says:

If there is righteousness in the heart
There will be beauty in the character
If there is beauty in the character
There will be harmony in the home.
When there is harmony in the home
There will be order in the nation.
When there is order in the nation,
There will be peace in the world.

(*Sathya Sai Speaks,* 7, pp. 189-90)

The last gem of golden ray serene is non-violence which is closely connected with the other four: Truth, *Dharma,* Love and Peace. It seems that Baba has composed a symphony of the traditional moral virtues coming from ancient times and glorified by all religions, prophets and various incarnations of the Lord. These values are traditional, but have universal appeal and the acquisition of each or all of them carves out the destiny of man in the very image of God. That is why I have described them as gems or priceless treasures. Man looks before and after and pines for what is not. He goes in search of spiritual treasures in the wilderness of the material world, little knowing that the gems are all buried in his back garden. These gems shine brilliantly and radiate their golden rays serene all round and are repository of radiance and splendour like that imperial planet, the sun. If one is asked to point out the basic and integral teaching of Bhagwan Sri Sathya Sai Baba, it will not be wrong to say that the five moral virtues or human values with their diamond-like hardness, transparency and serene luminosity constitute the crux and the kernel of his message.

The last, but not the least of the human values, is non-violence or *ahimsa.* It has close kinship with love, truth, peace and righteousness. Non-violence is the attitude of the mind that leads people to live in perfect harmony and kinship with others. At the same time, non-violence presupposes high degree of faith and belief in truth and right action. For practical purposes, non-violence is an attitude of the mind when one avoids causing or inflicting pain on others. It implies strict adherence to truth and morality. In the words of Baba,

> *Ahimsa* (non-violence) is another phase of truth. When once you are aware of the kinship, the oneness in God, the fundamental *Atmic* unity, no one will knowingly cause pain or distress to another.
>
> (*Sathya Sai Speaks,* 1, p. 128)

The safest rule to follow is the injunction 'Do unto others, what you would have them do unto you.' Thus, non-violence must be a part of our perceptions and outlook. However, in doing one's duty one may be called upon to do harm to others. In performance of his duty a policeman may have to harm a criminal. A soldier in the battle-field may have to annihilate the enemy. There are different standards of judgment. A dacoit who murders a person may be said to have committed violence; whereas a surgeon who amputates a part of the patient's body to save his life is just doing his rightful duty as surgeon. Lord Krishna, who was an apostle of peace, encouraged prince Arjuna to wage a war against the *Kauravas* to vanquish the evil for the greater good of the society and lasting peace in the world. Baba has very nicely stated:

> Krishna wanted the peace of the world and yet he encouraged the big battle in which forty lakhs of people were killed. Is this *himsa* (violence) or *ahimsa* (non-violence)? Even then Krishna gave an appropriate answer to this. He said, 'Arjuna, let us take the case of a cancerous growth of the body, and this cancerous growth gives pain to the whole human body, although the growth itself is confined to a

> localized area. In this battle or the operation, forty lakhs of disease-causing germs will be killed for the benefit of the world. Is this bad or is this for the good of the world?'

Sathya Sai Baba illustrates further:

> The meaning of *ahimsa* is that either in thought, deed, or word, you should not cause harm to anybody. Gandhi took a vow that until the end of his life, he would follow this. But on one occasion when he saw a cow suffering from pain, he could not bear it and he advised the doctor to give an injection and end the life of the cow. Thus, in order to help the suffering individual, we may sometimes have to harm him.
>
> (Sathya Sai Baba, *Summer Showers*, 1977, p. 235)

Thus, non-violence is beautiful and resplendent gem of golden ray serene; the acquisition of this priceless treasure may transform the life of the practitioner into a saga of peace and love and bring him closer to God. *Ahimsa* is integral with the other highly cherished and desirable virtues that are the essential ingredients for a virtuous and meaningful existence on this planet.

This author has used the analogy of music to explain the significance of these five moral principles in his work, *Sai Baba: The Rose-Fire of Heaven*. A quartet is chamber music played within the chamber in which four instruments constitute the ensemble. The distinctive mark of a quartet is that the four instruments are played on simultaneously. While the one is played, the other three are continually and concurrently heard. This creates a fugue as opposed to a solo or a symphony; and the music is heard so deeply that it is not heard at all! The five instruments or notes, *sathya, dharma, prema, shanthi* and *ahimsa,* constitute the ensemble and each is conterminus with the other. Swami says that if one practises a single of these virtues honestly and truthfully in one's daily life, the other four will automatically be his own possession.

At this stage, it may be fair to refer to the medieval quest romances in which the romance hero or the questor has been projected as a paragon of virtue. Thus we have a Sir Galhad, Sir Percival, Sir Gawan and the Green Knight and numerous others. King Arthur and his knights of the round table are all paragons of chivalry and courtesy. They are noble and pure-hearted persons whose chief loyalty is to their country and to their lady-love. They perform deeds of courage and valour so as to please their lady-love and prove themselves to be worthy of their noble calling as knights. They are not tainted by any radical defect in their character and are emblems of courtesy, valour and purity. In the process of their quest, they undertake the perilous journey to the Grail castle and encounter the Grail girl who asks them a number of questions. On giving the correct answers to these questions, they can get the mythical and symbolic grail and are ultimately united with the Grail girl which is the ultimate goal of all their quest. King Arthur has been described as the ideal knight. Even in Spenser's *The Faerie Queene,* the main task of the Renaissance poet is to fashion a gentleman in the noble and virtuous disciplines. In this moral allegory, each knight represents a particular moral discipline, such as holiness, chastity, friendship etc. And Prince Arthur represents the twelve moral virtues as described by Plato, Plotinus and in *Nichomacean Ethics.* He is the very epitome of perfection and purity. He may be the exponent of magnificence which may be termed as the supreme virtue combining all others in a grand design. *The Faerie Queene* is a fable, a romance and an allegory which operates on three different planes of meaning, the literal, the romantic and the moral or spiritual. By the same token, the priceless gems offered by Bhagwan Sri Sathya Sai Baba are aimed at the noble ideal of fashioning out the spiritual quest of mankind. Once we imbibe the golden rays of *sathya, dharma,* love, peace and non-violence and make them the mentor and guide of our daily living, thought, word and deed, we shall march with confidence to our avowed destination of merging with the infinite, supreme Ray of the universe, because that Absolute Eternal can be known only through adherence to these five ways of *knowing.*

The central teachings of Sri Sathya Sai Baba are strongly reminiscent of the perennial Indian philosophy and have a remarkable one-to-one correspondence with the *Sermon on the Mount* preached by Jesus Christ. We might even discern a close similarity between the main teachings of Jesus Christ and those of Sri Sathya Sai Baba. This may largely be on account of the fact that there is a basic and essential unity of all religions and that the incarnations of the Absolute Eternal think alike. In Christian theology, there is a prime emphasis on love, truth, charity and compassion and on non-violence.

In *Koran* and Buddhistic religious texts we again find great stress on the five-fold path of moral and spiritual regeneration. Of course, there are differences of presentment of these eternal verities depending on the individual distinctive factors and the compulsions of time and clime. The techniques and modes of presentation are bound to differ depending upon the personal outlook and genius of the teacher. For instance, Jesus Christ, who spoke to the crowds, used parables to drive home the message effectively to his audience. Sai Baba has striking resemblance with Jesus Christ so far as his mode of delivering his sermons is concerned inasmuch as he makes copious use of parables, figures of speech, analogies and homely illustrations. And, it becomes apparent as we hear him, that he hammers his points persistently to convince us and there is always a tough reasonableness beneath the lyric grace of his poetic and often impassioned discourses. Even those who do not understand Telugu seem to be swayed by the rhetoric of his speech and the music of his oration. It may safely be presumed that Baba is a poet, a great poet that only God can be. He has all the resources of language, speech, gesture and intonation and rhythm which result in the rhythmic expansion of his message and meaning beyond the limitations of time and space. Apart from the five gems of golden ray serene, there are many a facet of the divine diamond that require attention. Baba has declared that the first sixteen years of his life will be devoted to *mahima* and the next sixteen years to miracles and that the remaining years will be devoted to *upadesa* or preaching sermons but at the same time, he has said that *mahimas,* miracles and *upadesa* would continue together.

Some of the salient features of Sai Baba's teachings have to be highlighted because they provide the basis for the salvation of mankind by offering the true perspective for spiritual progress. Baba is never tired of hammering out the point that man is pure *atma,* a fragment of the *paramatma* which is his true and real home; as such man has to ultimately return to his divine origin and strive to seek merger with the Absolute. The body of man is no more than a temporary and temporal vestment. The *atma* resident in the body is formless, but it creates the forms it requires. It creates five sheaths in the body, namely, *anamayakosha, paramanayakosha, manomayakosha, vijnamayakosha* and finally, *anandamayakosha.* Baba stresses the point that in order to reach the stage of liberation and beatitude, man must get rid of earthly desires and attachments. This, according to Baba, involves long and continuous *sadhana.* Baba says that to get immersed in the Eternal Absolute one has to fully understand the *atma* principle, the divinity within, and if this is achieved, man can become God by merging his soul with the universal *atma* or *paramatma.* It follows from this that the basis of love and brotherhood of man is the truth of the *Atma* principle. When you come to realize that God resides in everyone, all feeling of separateness vanishes. Baba uses the analogy of the electricity current. The same current flows through everyone.

The other important teaching of Sai Baba has to do with the nature, existence and immanence of the Divine principle. Although God is formless, he manifests himself in any form. In his famous pronouncement Baba has said:

> There is only one caste, the caste of humanity; there is only one religion, the religion of love; there is only one God and he is omnipresent.
>
> (Sathya Sai Baba)

According to Sri Sathya Sai Baba, God is without form or formless.

The Lord can be addressed by any name that tastes sweet to your tongue, or pictured in any form that appeals to your sense of wonder and awe. You can sing of him as Maruga, Ganpathi, Sarada, Jesus, Maitreyi, Sakti or you can call him Allah or the Formless, or the Master of all Forms. It makes no difference at all. He is the beginning, the middle and the end, the basis, the substance and the source. Baba says that God is nearer to us than our hands and feet. We don't have to search for him beyond the starry constellations, for the loving merciful God, our eternal charioteer, is ever close at hand and can rush to our rescue in moments of crisis provided the voice of our calling is sincere and prayerful. As Baba has reassured all: 'As the doctor is found where patients gather, so the Lord is ever with the suffering and the struggling...wherever people cry out for God, there God will be.' Baba's chief message to humanity is that exhorts mankind to reach and realize the divinity within through the exercise of love, truth, peace and non-violence and selfless service to all. Baba does not prescribe a life of ceaseless penance in a cave or in the mountains by renouncing the world. Rather he advises us to lead the ordinary life in the world and yet engage ourselves in spiritual practices without being bound to the attachments and allurements of the world. Baba gives the analogy of a boat on the crest of the tempestuous seas. A boat cruises on water, but the water must not get into the boat. Similarly, one must live in the world, but the world must not get into one. Giving another analogy of a drama, Baba says that the world is a puppet show in which one has to act one's roles, but one should not identify oneself with the shadow play and must steer clear of the temporal and the insubstantial and must always remember that he is the child of immortality and has the power to discriminate between appearance and reality, shadow and substance.

Sathya Sai Baba also points out the need for following the pathways of *yoga* for disciplining the mind and moving towards the divine centre. These paths of enlightenment have been prescribed in the *sanatan dharma.* They are known as *Karma yoga, Jnana yoga* and *Bhakthi yoga.* Baba says:

> Base your action on knowledge, the knowledge that all is one. Let the action be suffused with *bhakthi,* that is to say, humility, mercy and non-violence. Let *bhakthi* be filled with knowledge, otherwise it will be as light as a balloon which drifts along any current of air or gust of wind. Mere knowledge will make the heart dry, *bhakthi* makes it soft with sympathy and *karma* gives the hands something to do, something which will sanctify every one of the minutes that have fallen to your lot to live.
>
> (Sathya Sai Baba)

Baba has described the three lanes of spiritual realization in a perfectly convincing manner. As Howard Murphet has said:

> I once heard Baba talk of these three lanes to self-realization. He called them the three Ws, work, worship and wisdom. Work (*karma*) alone is, he said, a slow passenger train with long stops and some changes at junctions before you reach the end of the journey. But if you add *bhakthi* to work, you will have an express coach and get in your destination more quickly and easily. Work and worship together will furthermore develop wisdom or the knowledge of the real (*jnana*). With this you will then be in a non-stop train right to the end of your journey. So worship while you work and strive meanwhile for the self-knowledge that will help these two to bring the true wisdom.
>
> (Howard Murphet, *Sai Baba: Man of Miracles*, p. 195)

The beauty and the power of Sai Baba's teachings lie in their instant and immediate appeal to our mind because they are clothed in simple and homely medium and have the weight and sanction of the true voice of feeling. Baba talks to his audience as man to man and, of course, as *sadguru*, a world teacher who is also a world redeemer like Jesus Christ. The central thrust of his teachings is that we must aspire to reach a level of consciousness where all is one and the same divinity is there entrenched in the hearts of all. One must seek God through ardour, selflessness and self-surrender. And to achieve this kind of supreme effacement of the ego, one has to undergo the difficult exercise of a lifetime's death in love, ardour and selflessness and self-surrender. Baba's teachings are neither abstract nor metaphysical like the teachings of some doctrinaire philosophers or religious theologians of different faiths; they are remarkably plastic and concrete, practical and empirical in the extreme. Sai Baba, in his Shirdi body, had given his devotees some important and crucial hints for God realization, and Sri Sathya Sai Baba has also been hammering on these points in his discourses. These in a nutshell can be simplified to absolute formulae:

> The spiritual aspirant must realize the absolute triviality and insignificance of things material and worldly, worldly

honours, laurels and titles. His aim must be higher, that is to turn his gaze inwards and discover the divinity within which is the mirror reflection of the God himself. He must always follow the master, his conscience, the indwelling God.

The aspirant must control his mind and his senses. If the mind is unrestrained and senses unmanageable, like wild and vicious horses drawing a chariot, he cannot reach his destination. The mind should not only be controlled, it must also be purified to be a vessel of divine love.

Finally, the most important thing is that one must have the grace of the Lord without which nothing can be attained.

The teachings of Lord Krishna in the *Srimad Bhagwat Gita* and those of Shirdi Baba and Sri Sathya Sai Baba have the same universal quality. They represent the concentrated essence of all that the Vedas, Upanisads, Puranas and Bible have taught.

Sri Sathya Sai Baba has emphasized the fact that in the present age, *Kaliyuga,* the remembrance of the Lord's name is enough to lead man to the path of self-realization, and *bhakthi marg* is the easiest to practise. He lays stress on the fact that a true seeker must lead a life of absolute devotion to truth, love, peace and non-violence and steer clear of all impurities, falsehoods, and crazy attachments to worldly desires. We know that in his Fire Sermon, Lord Buddha also has preached the gospel of desirelessness, the burning out of all base passions, attachments and temptations so as to reach the cherished goal of attaining *Nirvana.*

In his conversations with John Hislop, Swami has clarified many points about the essential unity of everyone in the divine tapestry.

Hislop: When does one really experience that he is the same as another? Because, now one feels for another through compassion. But compassion is not direct experience. When someone hit a dog, Shirdi Sai Baba had the bruises. That is the actual experience of unity.

Sai: All is divine. When you are firmly established in the fact of your divinity, then you will directly know that others are divine. Compassion for others is felt as long as you consider yourself as a separate entity. The story about Shirdi Sai Baba as related in books is not fully correct. The facts are that a lady made a plate of sweets for Shirdi Baba, and a dog ate them. The lady drove the dog away with blows. She then carried another platter of sweets to Shirdi Baba, who refused them saying that he had eaten the sweets she previously provided and his hunger was satisfied. The lady objected that it was the first time the sweets had been offered. Baba said, no, she had offered them before and had also beaten him. In this way, he gave the lesson that he was omnipresent and that there was only one life. During the lifetime of Shirdi Baba not much attention was paid to him. Recognition of him as an *Avatar,* and interest in his life developed only after his death. The same lack of recognition of divinity is illustrated in the lives of Rama and Krishna. Krishna was considered just as a cowherd boy, and, then, just as a charioteer.

(*Conversations,* pp. 152-53)

Sai (at the start of an interview with a group of Westerners): Follow the master, the inside *atma,* the super conscious. Life is a challenge; fight to the end. Life is a song; sing it. Life is divine; realize it. Life is character; there is one path.

Sai (to a young Westerner about age 16): What do you want?

Boy: Liberation.

Sai: What is liberation?

Boy: End of the path.

Sai: Immortality is the meaning. Removal of immorality is the only way to immortality. Who are you? Not the outside, not the body. Who are you? Inquire. Love is everything. Expansion love, not selfish love. Selfless love of the Self, not Ego love...Life is a cosmic stage in which all are actors. In one scene an actor may take one role, and in other scenes, different roles. Creation means change. How can these changing scenes give bliss to persons who are also changing? Your bliss can be made permanent only by immortality, not change.

(*Conversations,* pp. 164-65)

Thus, in his conversations with John Hislop, Baba has thrown light on various topics, puzzling the minds of devotees. He has offered the most priceless gems that shine like golden rays of the sun and ever become part and parcel of our mental furniture.

Sai Baba has prescribed for the spiritual seekers many resplendent gems of golden ray serene which take us along the sunlit path of *sadhana* and self-enquiry and take us nearer to the end of our divine pilgrimage. In the last chapter of this book, an attempt will be made to analyze the various grounds of our beseeching and the different modes of our apprehension of the divine reality or the voice of our calling. But here, some broad hints have been listed whereby one can move on the straight path to heaven. Dr. Samuel Sandweiss has given in the following the precise contours of Sai Baba's central teachings which are the essential prerequisites for moving on the fateful pilgrimage to God.

> The nine steps in the pilgrimage of man towards God along the path of dedication and surrender are (1) developing a desire to listen to the glory and grandeur of God, the handiwork of God and the various awesome manifestations of God divinity. This is the starting point. It is hearing about the Lord again and again that we can transform ourselves into divinity. (2) Singing oneself about the Lord, in praise of his magnificence and many other exploits. (3) Dwelling on the Lord in the mind, revelling in the contemplation of his beauty, majesty and compassion. (4) Entering upon the worship of the Lord by concentrating on honouring the feet or the footprints.
>
> (5) This develops into a total propitiation of the Lord and systematic ritualistic worship in which the aspirant gets inner satisfaction and inspiration. (6) The aspirant begins to see the favourite form of God which he likes to worship, in all beings and all objects wherever he turns, and so he develops an attitude of *vandana* or reverence towards nature and all life. (7) Established in this bent of mind, he becomes the devoted servant of all, with no sense of superiority or inferiority. This is a vital step which presages great spiritual success.

(8) This takes the seeker so near the Lord that he feels himself to be confidant and comrade, the companion and friend, the sharer of God's power and pity, of God's triumphs and achievements, his *Sakha* in fact, as Arjuna had become. (9) As can be inferred, this is the prelude to the final step of total surrender or *atmanivedanam,* yielding fully to the will of the Lord, which the seeker knows through his own purified intuitions...One of the principles of straight living is silence, for the voice of God can be heard in the region of the heart only when the tongue is stilled and the storm is stilled and the waves are calm...silence is the speech of the spiritual seeker. Soft sweet speech is the expression of genuine love. Hate screeches, fear squeals, conceit trumpets. Love sings lullabys. It soothes. It applies balm. Practise the vocabulary of love, unlearn the language of hate and contempt...The second sign is cleanliness; not outer cleanliness alone, but, even more, inner. There is a strange glow on the face of a guileless person. Inner cleanliness has its own soap and water—the soap of strong faith and the water of constant practice. The third sign is that the true aspirant will have a reverent attitude to the duty he is bound with. He will carry out every task assigned to him as if it is the act of worship by which the Lord will be pleased, through which he can approach the pedestal of God. Work is worship—this is the motto...render every thought into a flower, worthy to be held in His fingers, render every deed into a fruit, full of the sweet juice of love, fit to be placed in His hand, render every tear holy and pure, fit to wash His lotus feet...

(*Sathya Sai Speaks,* 7, pp. 195-98)

Obviously, Sai Baba has given the recipe for leading a straight and pious life lived under the shadow of the divine in consonance with the awareness of divine presence. This is what the spiritual path is all about. Baba goes on to say adherence to these golden rules can confer permanent bliss on the seeker won through self-control and self-realization. Baba says:

Do not judge others to decide whether they deserve your

service. Find out only whether they are distressed: that is enough credential. Do not examine how they behave towards others, they can be certainly transformed by love *Sewa* or service is for you as sacred a vow as *Sadhana*, a spiritual path. It is the very breath, it can only end when breath takes leave of you.

(*Sathya Sai Speaks, 7,* pp. 195-98)

One can say in conclusion that there are many a ray of golden ray serene that are hidden in the basic core of one's being. One can dig them up by developing an attitude of independent self-inquiry. Such an attitude comes naturally to us since our basic nature is love, purity and reverence. If we follow the nine basic steps formulated by Baba and live a virtuous life based on *sathya, dharma, prema, shanthi* and *ahimsa,* we can travel the path leading to the celestial city of God.

Not only in his conversations with John Hislop, but also in his numerous interviews given to different groups of western devotees, Sri Sathya Sai Baba has clarified many points relating to the practice of the spiritual path. These suggestions are, in a different sense, illuminations which sharpen the focus on the essential quest of reaching the state of supreme bliss, Being, Awareness and Bliss. Here are some of the relevant excerpts that throw a flood of light on the attendant modes of *sadhana* or spiritual practice.

Devotee: Baba. Please tell us how you are attained. I find my *sadhana* (spiritual practice) unproductive.

Sai Baba: I know you are inflicting many austerities on yourself. I must tell you I am attained only by devotion and a way of life that is illumined by that devotion. Do not deprive the body of the elementary needs, it is a sacred instrument you have earned, for taking you to the goal. Lead a simple, *satwic* (balanced, pure, good) life, eat simple *satwic* food, be sincere in speech, do loving service, be humble and tolerant. Maintain undisturbed equanimity. Direct all your thoughts towards me, resident in your heart.

Devotee: How, Baba, can we progress in our devotion?

Sai Baba: There are different modes of devotion: that which foolishly weeps for me when I am not physically present; that which surrenders to me with wild abandon; and that which is steady and strong, ever attached to my will. I accept all these forms of devotion. The choice between the one or the other is not yours, because it is I who rules your feelings, modifies them. If you try to go where I do not will, you can do nothing apart from my will. Be assured of that, this is the highest devotion.

Devotee: So what remains for me to do?

Sai Baba: What makes you think that doing is so important? Be equal-minded. Then you will not be bothered about doing or not doing, success or failure. The balance will remain unaffected by either. Let the wave of memory, the storm of desire, the fire of emotion pass through without affecting your equanimity. Be a witness to these. Commitment engenders holding, narrowing, limiting. Be willing to be nothing. Let all dualities subside in your neutrality.

Devotee: Yes, Baba. But when it is pain that one has to endure...

Sai Baba: Do you think that I would confront you with pain were there not a reason for it? Open your heart to pain, as you do now for pleasure, for it is my will, wrought by me for your good. Welcome it as a challenge. Do not turn away from it. Do not listen to your mind, for mind is but another word for need. The mind engenders need; it manifested as this world because it needed this. It is all my plan: to drive you by pangs of unfulfilled need to listen to my voice, which, when heard, dissolves the ego and the mind with it.

Devotee: But being full of defects, how can we rise to such high expectations?

Sai Baba: Your deficiencies make you need me and curb the arrogance of your mind. They are there on purpose, as instruments to prod you on. Through them, I am making you want me. The feeling of separation is just a trick of your mind. You form conclusions; they become beliefs, they shape your activities and attitudes.

Devotee: It is hard to undergo your tests.

> Sai Baba: It is like baking a cake. I stir, I knead, I pound, I twist, I bake you. I drown you in tears; I scorch you in sobs. I make you sweet and crisp, an offering worthy of God. I have come to reform you. My plan is to transmute you into a successful *sadhaka* (spiritual aspirant). I won't leave you until I do that. Even if you stray away before you become that, I will hold on to you. You cannot escape from me...All are my instruments. Perhaps you believe that I choose: this one is good...that one is worse, etc. No. Either will do. My will is the source of all that is and happens, it interpenetrates every thing and act; it includes everything. Finally, let me tell you this: My will is that you should manifest my will in you and through you.
>
> (Sathya Sai Baba, *Sanathan Sarathi*, August 1974, p. 185)

Lastly, before this particular chapter on the priceless pearls of golden ray serene is terminated, it may be fair to quote the important observation of Sathya Sai Baba in respect of the spiritual exercise as a means of the purification of one's motives and to see the one single flame that is inclusive of the entire cosmos, substance and weight, as together fused into the blazing light of the single flame.

> Sai: The purpose of all *sadhana* is to see the good the Divine in everything and to be able to overlook the bad, the evil. From the viewpoint of Divinity, there is no good or bad — all is Divine. But the mind sees this as good and that as bad, this as right and that as wrong. It is the mind that must be trained to see the Divine in everyone and in each difficulty ...Do not fill the mind with thoughts of the evil actions that may be perceived in the world. The purpose of all types of *sadhana* is to see the Divine in everything. This is true adjustment *sadhana.* This you can carry on in everything you do.
>
> (*Conversations*, pp. 200-01)

Thus, we have taken a measure of some of the precious gems beyond all price that are and can be our precious acquisitions and possessions once we voyage on the path of *atmic sadhana* and spiritual exploration for the attainment of the true purpose of our life.

8

THE RAY SUPREME AND THE VOICE OF OUR CALLING

As Jonathan Roof has rightly observed, the present age and this moment of human history is of the greatest and momentous significance. In his own words,

> For aspirants whose intuitive vision is open, this is a time of great opportunity. The *poorna* Avatar of the *Kaliyuga* is now incarnate as Sri Sathya Sai Baba. He has come possessed of the sixteen attributes and physical signs foretold in past ages. He manifests the energy and powers of a superhuman being, yet some observers are still unsure of his stature. On occasions, he pretends not to know the visitor or where the visitor comes from, but that is his play. The devotee must overcome this the illusion which blinds him to the magnificent reality.
>
> (Jonathan Roof, *Pathways to God,* p. 20)

Sai Baba has also cautioned the people not to be swayed by *maya* or delusion but to catch the fleeting glimpses of the divine whenever they have a chance to do so. Baba says:

> Since I move about with you, eat like you, and talk with you, you are deluded into the belief that this is but an instance of common humanity. Be warned against this mistake. I am also deluding you by my singing with you, talking with you, and by engaging myself in activities with you. But any moment, my divinity may be revealed to you. You have to be ready, prepared for that moment. Since divinity is enveloped with humaneness, you must overcome the *maya*

(delusion) that hides it from your eyes.

(*Sathya Sai Speaks*, 6, p. 211)

Unlike the past ages, the present age is an age of rank scepticism and of the lost dimensions of belief. So, the incarnation of the age has come to educate and lift all humanity by his mission of love, peace, righteousness and non-violence. Not only this, he has set up his own example in the manner of Rama and Krishna, Jesus Christ and the Buddha. Sri Sathya Sai Baba is truly the guide and example for the *Kaliyuga*. There are certain ways in which the advent of an incarnation can benefit humanity, the only condition is that one should be prepared to follow the guidelines set by him and walk the straight path, that is the great highway to God. Baba says:

> The way in which the *Avatar* has to be used for one's liberation and uplift is: watch his every step, observe his actions and activities, follow the guiding principles of which his life is an elaboration. Mark his love, his compassion, his wisdom and try to bring them into your own life.

(*Sathya Sai Speaks*, 6, pp. 166-67)

One of the tasks of the present *Avatar* is the deliverance of all those who have earned the right of liberation or *mukthi* from the ceaseless whirlpool and cycle of birth and death. Baba gives the analogy of an aeroplane:

> The airplane has to land at certain places in order to take those who have won the right to fly by the tickets they have purchased. So, too, the Lord has come down that those who have won the right to be liberated may be saved; incidentally, others too will know of the Lord, of his grace, of ways of winning it, of the joy of liberation.

(*Sathya Sai Speaks*, 4, p. 24)

Verily the *Avatar* is a ray from the Supreme, come to light the lamp of love and to illumine the hearts and souls of men and women; all one needs is to listen to him with reverence and learn the lessons taught by him, and obey him with love, hope and faith. It is as simple as that.

Since the light from above has descended on earth, it is our duty to bathe in the effulgence of its radiance, warmth and grace. If we miss this chance, there is no knowing when we shall get another chance.

Our great Lord Sathya Sai Baba is the very quintessence of the Divine principle. He is a loving and forgiving God, ever ready to stand by his devotees and true spiritual aspirants. There have been numerous instances of his deep compassion, profound pity and mercy. While engaged in running the cosmos and the entire universe, he takes time out to attend to the needs of his devotees whom he holds near and dear to himself as his very breath. He has expressed this in answer to a query from John Hislop:

> H.: Swami. We have just now actually witnessed a part of this amazing story. How can that all be? Swami holds the entire universe in his hand. He bears the responsibility of this inconceivably immense universe. And how can he, at the same time, give the detailed attention to the lives of individual devotees?
>
> Sai: It is as you say. Swami holds the universe in his hands. But devotees learn of the glory and majesty through Swami's attention to each one personally. That Swami holds the universe yet at the same time, fully cares for the lives of his devotees even to the smallest details is a measure of his glory that the devotees can understand.

(*Conversations,* p. 173)

The same point has been stressed again in a different context which illustrates the universal omnipresence, omniscience and omnipotence of Bhagwan Sri Sathya Sai Baba:

> H.: Baba has the inconceivably immense task of the universe. How can he afford to spend time talking to people like us?
>
> Sai: Baba, with his limitless bodies, is everywhere doing his tasks, a thousand heads, hands, feet — *Sahasra sheershaa purushah samraksha, sahasrapaad*—it is just this body that sits here talking to you. That is Baba's omnipresence. The *Avatar* is beyond the five elements. He is the Creator...God is not subject to any limitation. He is the creator of the elements, their modifier, their preserver, their destroyer...Baba means Being-Awareness-Bliss-one Reality.

(*Conversations,* pp. 89-90)

W.H. Mackintosh, a renowned British writer and intellectual who had the occasion to review Dr. Samuel Sandweiss' famous book *The Holy Man and the Psychiatrist,* has indeed taken a very empirical, rational and enlightened view of Sai Baba and his Reality and does not dispute the idea that Sai Baba may be, in reality, an *Avatar*. His comments are so illuminating that this author is tempted to quote it in full:

> The embodiment of deity in human form is a rare event, it happens only when the human condition has deteriorated to such an extent that nothing else can bring about a redemption. It cannot be denied that the present situation seems to demand an *Avatar's* appearance. Dr. Sandweiss, an American psychiatrist, is very much a man of the time. He is trained to regard the scientific method as the most consistently reliable way of reaching the truth, and is imbued with the tenets of modern psychology, which lays so much stress on the need to avoid repression. He seems to be an unlikely advocate of the spiritual discipline, which rejects the most cherished beliefs of contemporary materialism. Yet again and again, he had made pilgrimages to Bangalore to sit at the feet of Sai Baba and partake of this holy man's infinite wisdom. He found in Sai Baba a being whose nature and power were utterly incomprehensible to him. This was no ordinary *Guru,* a publicity-seeking Swami, but a Master about whom stories were told strangely reminiscent of Jesus, Buddha and Krishna.
>
> Is Sai Baba an *Avatar,* an incarnation of God? This is an important question that demands a considered answer. If he is an incarnation of God, he is the greatest being in the world and indeed the greatest being who could exist.
>
> Like others born and bred in a humanistic environment, I find the idea scarcely credible. I am bewildered and perplexed by the implications. I have lived long enough to learn a few lessons, not many perhaps, but sufficient in number and magnitude to convince me of the limitations of my understanding. I know too little either to affirm or deny the possibility of a miracle—and the incarnation of God would

> certainly be a miracle. We have no right to assert that the infinite intelligence cannot assume a finite embodiment of itself. For, if the attributes of divinity are omnipotence, omnipresence and omniscience, God's assumption of human shape is a very simple exercise of his power.
>
> However much my skeptical but limited intellect may want to reject the notion of an *Avatar*, the deeper insight into reality afforded by imagination and intuition does not allow me to deny that Sai Baba may indeed be an incarnation of God. Many witnesses testify to the extraordinary effect which Sai Baba's presence has on them. It is not the subtle influence of a God-intoxicated man but a much more powerful direct emanation and outflow of indescribable bliss which transforms the consciousness of those present.
>
> As I have never been in Sai Baba's presence I cannot assess the effect to which I have referred. But, as this book includes numerous quotations and extracts from his teachings, I can comment on their content and quality. The style in which they are written is clear and concise. As I read them I was conscious of an immediate impact which seemed to penetrate the very depth of my mind. The emphasis is always on God and his inexhaustible love.
>
> (Quoted by Samuel Sandweiss, *Spirit and the Mind*, pp. 38-39)

Of course, the review appears to be forthright and candid and may be said to represent view of the cross-section of a vast number of people who have not had the chance to experience Sai Baba; but the unending trek from far-flung corners of the globe continues and the recognition of the divinity of Sai Baba may become universal in course of time. As a general rule, the recognition of an *Avatar* during his lifetime is fraught with exceptional difficulty.

How many recognized Rama and Krishna as *Avatars* in their own times and how many considered Jesus Christ to be the son of God? Baba has himself thrown sufficient light on this problem, and we have to take his words in absolute faith. Baba says:

> On previous occasions when God incarnated on earth, the bliss of recognizing him in the incarnation was vouchsafed only after the physical embodiment had left the world, in spite of plenty of patent evidences of his Grace. And the loyalty and devotion they commanded from men arose through fear and awe at their superhuman power and skills, or their imperial and penal authority.
>
> (*Sathya Sai Speaks*, 6, p. 212)

And further, he has clarified that he had taken upon himself the responsibility of disclosing his divinity. Not only in his famous address delivered at the Sathya Sai World Conference in Bombay in 1968 but also on many other occasions he has been pleased to reiterate that point for the benefit of his devotees. He says:

> It is very difficult to demarcate clearly the manifestation of the Lord, so I am announcing myself, and am myself describing my mission, the task, the characteristics, the qualities that mark out the *Avatar* from the rest.
>
> (*Sathya Sai Speaks*, 4, p. 21)

Sri Sathya Sai Baba's answers to some of the intimate queries of John Hislop clarify many doubts in this regard.

> H.: It seems strange that only a few people recognize the *Avatar*.
>
> Sai: No, not strange! How would you know the *Avatar*?
>
> H.: By faith.
>
> Sai: Faith is one thing. Knowing is another...You know Swami as an *Avatar*?
>
> H.: Yes.
>
> Sai: No doubts?
>
> H.: No doubts, whatsoever.
>
> Sai: Your own experience is that Swami is omnipresent.
>
> H.: Yes, that is my direct experience.
>
> Sai: Yet when you leave Swami at Brindavan and arrive at your hotel you think of Swami as being at Brindavan. You see it is not easy to know the omnipresent *Avatar*. Of course,

> there are always some who know. In the Krishna *Avatar* there were some who knew. Likewise, there were some who knew the Rama *Avatar*. Not every blossom opens to the sun when it rises. Only some are ready. There is the factor of ripeness. Not every fruit on a tree is ripe at the same time.
>
> (*Conversations*, pp. 164-65)

That Sri Sathya Sai Baba is a Ray from the Supreme should no longer be called in question. The scientists with keenest intellect think that he is a phenomenon; the rationalists are simply confounded; the atheists and non-believers are dismayed and confused and begin to doubt their previous stance. But those who possess simple faith and natural intuition do not find it difficult to believe that there are many things on heaven and earth that philosophy cannot dream of. And God is such a thing. In this regard the attitude of Mr. Mackintosh seems to be most plausible and correct. One must wait until such time as the Divine showers his grace and the petals naturally open up to the sun. It seems quite fair to suggest that one should wait for the dawning of the light when, all on a sudden, the beloved face of God is revealed to one in a blaze of light. Most of the devotees of Sai Baba have had the glimpse of Baba's divinity and his calls have been unique and extraordinary. It is he who manifests his visiting cards in the shrines of potential devotees, all those who are destined to see him in this lifetime, and calls them unto himself by strange logic of circumstances. This author has absolutely no doubt about it as he has undergone the same pattern of initiation. This is quite legitimate also as, like Christ, he first loved us and, then, kindled the flame of that love within us.

The experience of Allen S. Levy, recorded in *Transformation of the Heart,* ed. by Judy Warner, deserves to be mentioned here because it is typical of how incessant and compulsive the call of Baba can be.

> I walked up the three flights of stairs of the dilapidated building, a dark contrast to the upper middle class home in which my brother and I had grown up. I knocked on the door at the head of the stairs, and a tall young man answered. In spite of my grave doubts, he confirmed that

this was indeed my brother's place.

I could smell a flowery essence wafting towards me from the interior, I could hear the strangest music, music so joyous that it filled me with a feeling of sheer delight. I danced into the apartment, moving in little circles, Jewish style, hand held high above my head. Reaching my brother's bedroom, I greeted him, 'Hi, Lou.' He was sitting on the floor on a mat, which, I was startled to learn, he called his bed, and burst into laughter at seeing me so happy (a strange occurrence), doing an even stranger dance in the middle of the room.

'What are you doing?' He asked.

I enthusiastically replied, 'I'm so happy. I can't help but dance. This music is wonderful. Who is it?'

Lou responded, 'Oh, that's Sai Baba singing *bhajans*.'

'Who's he?' I asked.

His reply threw me off a loop. 'He's God. He lives in India.'

'God. What God? The one in your fantasies? Come on!'

Lou's response hit me right where my stubborn intellect was most vulnerable. 'See for yourself. Read about him.'

Lou gave me a book, *Baba* by Arnold Schulman. Within a few days I reluctantly opened it, and read. After ten pages I put the book down, my mind numb. In fact, my mind seemed to have stopped—an impossible occurrence especially for me. After a few all too brief moments it began again but all I could think was 'Oh! God. This is God.' In a state of sheer excitement, I picked up the phone, dialled my brother. 'Lou, you're right! This is God. Sathya Sai Baba is God. What do I do now?'

He calmly replied, 'Relax. Sit down and meditate. When I see you next we'll talk more about it. Keep reading.'

This was the beginning, and I may add, only the beginning of magnificent, munificent grace which Baba would shower upon me.

(Allen S. Levy, 'It's all God', *Transformation of the Heart*, ed. Judy Warner, pp. 45-46)

We also have on record the experience of Walter Cowan who used to make astral travels and return to the body; but one day he was lost in the astral plane and found difficulty in returning to the body. But he was rescued by a benevolent figure. Later, when he saw the photograph of Baba on the title cover of Howard Murphet's book *Sai Baba: Man of Miracles,* he at once recognized his helper and benefactor. And from that day onwards, the Cowan couple became the most ardent devotees of Sai Baba. Even in the case of the present author, when life had become a saga of perpetual crisis and torments, the visit of a research student and her offer of a coloured portrait of Sai Baba set off a series of incredible events cementing the author's staunch faith in Baba's divinity. Such instances can be multiplied. But it is all the handiwork of the Divine father and mother to collect his children and open up the sunlit and rose-lit avenues of paradise.

So, we come to the inevitable conclusion that the present is the most exciting period of human history to live in as the sacred and hallowed time of *Tretayuga* and *Dwaparyuga* when Rama and Krishna incarnated on earth. And in *Kaliyuga,* the self-same divinity has made its appearance in all its fullness as Sri Sathya Sai Baba.

The question asked by Allen S. Levy seems to be quite relevant:

> 'Yes, He's God. Sathya Sai Baba is God. So, what do I do now?'

She found the answer in the teachings of Sai Baba as detailed below. She describes in her own words:

> In the following year while reading his books called *Sathya Sai Speaks,* Volumes I, II, III, etc. in the midst of a treasury of teachings, I came across what I thought as a most practical one for an overworked college student. 'The fruit of action belongs to the actor; therefore, renounce the fruit. Act, but renounce the fruit of the action; dedicate every action to God and renounce all desire for the fruit; call upon God to be the doer of action, and totally and fully, without recourse, renounce every vestige of attachment to the fruit of action.'
>
> (*Transformation of the Heart,* ed. Judy Warner, p. 46)

And, strangely enough, this formula worked for her miraculously. She had to write a final paper on American Civil Rights Movement and Black Political Thought and was stuck up. So, she resolved to retreat to her brother's apartment, and she narrates:

> Thanksgiving eve I sat down, paper on desk, pen in hand, and lit a candle before a picture of Sai Baba. I prayed: 'Oh God, It's Al Levy calling. Can you please write this paper on black political thought for me? You are the doer of all deeds, the speaker of all words, the thinker of all thoughts. Please, then, write this paper and bear the fruits. I surrender this all to you. Thanks.'
>
> For the next sixteen hours or so, he wrote. Every time I seemed to reach an impasse, I called Baba for help, praying as I had done before.
>
> (*Transformation of the Heart*, p. 47)

Not only this, Allen S. Levy was able to write her doctoral thesis by calling upon Baba to write the thesis for her as he was the doer of all deeds, speaker of all words and thinker of all thoughts and surrendering everything to him and asking him to bear the fruit of action. It follows from this that Allen S. Levy has been the exemplar of the highest type of *Sadhana,* taught by Lord Krishna and Sri Sathya Sai Baba about the need for disinterested action and complete surrender to the Lord without any attachment for the fruit of the action. But, apart from *Karma yoga* there are other ways of knowing and the method has to be adopted by a devotee strictly in accordance with his state of spiritual development and the ground of his beseeching. Apparently, his *atmanivedan* to the Lord would depend exclusively on these variable factors.

What we call the voice of our calling is, broadly speaking, the surge of feeling rising in the inner core of our hearts to adore the divine and merge with the great God. And whichever path we take, the central urge or the dominant passion to immerse in the Supreme Godhead remains basically the same. As T.S. Eliot says in the final movement of *Four Quartets,*

If you came this way,
Taking any route, starting from anywhere,
At any time or any season
It would always be the same.

And, the quest for the eternal reality is never-ending:

We shall never cease from exploration
And the end of our exploring
Will be to arrive where we started
And know the place for the first time.

This, indeed, is the burden of the quest. Only through the pilgrimage of love can one envision the radiant face of the beloved who is the Supreme Being, without beginning and end. The journey to the still centre becomes a distinct possibility. His anchor and hope is love. Now the light falls on a secluded chapel in Little Gidding as on the minarets of the temple at Prasanthi Nilayam and the seeker knows the place for the first time:

Through the unknown remembered gate
When the last of the earth left to discover
In that which was the beginning;
and the source of the longest river
The voice of the hidden waterfall.
And the children in the apple tree
Not known, because not looked for
But, heard, half-heard in the stillness
Between two waves of the sea.

(T.S. Eliot, *Four Quartets,* p. 39)

But the trouble is that for most of us the vision of the Divine is not vouchsafed or even if it is the moment is lost in the shaft of sunlight. However, the matter is entirely different for saints:

But to apprehend the intersection of Time
With the timeless is the occupation of the saint,
Not occupation either but something
Given and taken in a lifetime's death in love,
ardour and selflessness and self-surrender.

Thus, we see there is Raj Rani Mira who loved Krishna from the very core of her heart right from her angel infancy and even after she was married to the King, she did not swerve away from her constant devotion to her eternal beloved, Krishna.

Sai Baba of Shirdi has also said that the true disciple of the Lord thinks of nothing else except the Lord always and at all times. For him life without the presence of the Lord has no meaning whatsoever. This is what true devotion is all about. Even Sathya Sai Baba tells his devotees to yearn for him. This yearning is the motivating force behind infinite love.

Since the basic assumption in this work is that Bhagwan Sathya Sai Baba is a Ray from the Supreme and is a full *Avatar* of *Kaliyuga*, it becomes the duty of each individual to crave for him, and express deep reverence, ardour and yearning for him. What follows in the rest of the chapter is a blueprint for showing the profundity of our devotion and ways to give a full-throated expression of the resonance and power of the voice of our calling.

Let us start with a prayer which has been penned by none other than Sathya Sai Baba himself. This is a poem, instinct with the feelings of deathless love and complete devotion to the Lord. This is a prayer, phrased in profoundly moving imagery and metaphors which find an echo in our hearts:

Prayer

Oh Lord. Take my love and let it flow
In fullness of devotion to Thee.
Oh Lord. Take my hands and let them work
Incessantly for Thee.
Oh Lord. Take my soul and let it be
Merged in one with Thee.
Oh Lord. Take my mind and thoughts and
Let them be in tune with Thee.
Oh Lord. Take my everything and let
Me be an instrument to work for Thee.

With love and grace,

Baba

This prayer was written by Baba for use by the hostel students at the Sathya Sai colleges. This may be said to express the innermost feelings and sentiments of the tender and pure-hearted boys and girls who love Baba from the very core of their hearts. But, even the grown-ups, who live at faraway places and have faith in Baba, can conveniently use this prayer and find the exercise fairly wholesome and rewarding. Assuming that the *Avatar* is with us and we have the freedom to have his *darshan,* to speak to him and even touch his lotus feet, we can voice our sincerest prayers and supplications to him and work out our salvation with diligence. In this sense, we are very fortunate because the physical form of the *Avatar* can be seen by us, and the voice of our calling can be heard by him. If we pray to God, it poses some problems and difficulties. It requires a sense of non-dualism and complete identification with everything, the beauty and splendour of the universe. God is without form, but we know him through his creation. We know of his love and wisdom by seeing his beauty around us. As our divine vision grows, we begin to see God in everything. He is the essence of the self and everything that exists. God is ultimately formless, but we perceive him through form. Only through shape, colour and size can God be known. As Baba says:

> The *Sadhana* (spiritual discipline) can be to realize God as formless (*nirguna*) or with form (*saguna*). When one walks, the right foot and the left are both necessary. You cannot hop long on one foot. The *saguna sadhana* and *nirguna sadhana* are as the two feet.
>
> (*Sathya Sai Speaks,* 6, p. 26)

However, if we are face to face with the entity in whom all the attributes of the divine are concentrated, our devotion becomes much more tangible, concrete and convincing than in our supplication to the *Nirguna Brahman.*

The first requisite for our loving approach to the Divine essence is faith which goes on deepening with the progress in one's spiritual *sadhana.* When the edifice of faith is laid down firmly on unshakable foundation, one proceeds further by cementing it through remembrance of the name, keeping company of the good and the holy, devotion, meditation, self-surrender, song and service which is the gift of love. Indeed it is love that is the quintessence of all. As Baba has pointed out:

> Love in action is right action; as speech is truth; as thought is peace; as understanding is non-violence.
>
> (Sathya Sai Baba)

And we know that *Sathya, Dharma, Prema, Shanthi* and *Ahimsa* are the five priceless gems that Baba would like humanity to possess as the true facets of character. And Baba also assures each and everyone of us of his grace. He says:

> You may wonder, 'Why would God pay any attention to me? What could I possibly offer to Him that He would accept when the entire cosmos is already His? If even angels and Gods cannot see Him, what chance is there for me?' But such demeaning and belittling thoughts will get you nowhere. As long as you think this way, you will be unable to earn the grace of God and be fit to serve Him. Give no place to such displays of weakness. You must install God in your heart and say to Him 'Beloved Lord. I know you occupy the entire universe, but you are also here in my heart. With all my power I will keep you here, firmly established within me. You are, it is true, the greatest of the great but you are also the smallest of the small. In that minute aspect you reside always in my heart.' If you have this firm faith in yourself and a steadfast resolve to fix God unalterably in your heart, you will surely attain Him.
>
> (Sathya Sai Baba)

It follows from this that faith is the most invincible factor that takes one to the summit of belief and engenders the momentum of the whole spiritual journey. Verily, faith springs from self-understanding and awareness of one's inner divinity. This internal source or the *Atma* is the motivator and is a spring of courage and self-confidence. As Sathya Sai Baba has rightly pointed out,

> ...You believe in yourself because yourself is God and have an unshakable faith in God, deep down in you. Faith in yourself and faith in God are identical. You tap the strength of the God within when you stand attention against an enemy without.
>
> (*Sathya Sai Speaks*, 2, p. 229)

Knowledge comes from experience, but first we must act on faith. Baba says that faith is a tender plant that must be guarded so that it grows into a big tree. Faith can work wonders and can even impel the Lord to manifest himself. Baba has very nicely stated that faith in God is vital for the security and well being of the individual:

> Faith in God is the secure foundation on which hope has to be built. The faith has to be stable and strong. The feeling that God will come to our rescue has to be vivid and vital, motivating and activating all that we do or speak or think.
>
> (*Sathya Sai Speaks*, 7, p. 232)

What we call the voice of our calling is, for all practical purposes, the discipline of prayer. It is prayer that works miracles and is the royal road leading to victory. The sceptic and the atheist may question the validity of prayer and dismiss it as a figment of imagination. Here two things are of vital consideration. Does prayer actually work? Is the voice of our calling to God Almighty phrased properly and does it ring with the true voice of feeling? And the basic thing is, as we have seen, whether one has strong faith in God and his absolute power. If the answer of all these is in the affirmative, there is no doubt that the prayer will work, if not to the extent one imagines, at least it brings one closer to God. In the words of Sai Baba,

> Prayer is the very breath of religion, for it brings man and God together, and with every sigh, nearer and nearer.
>
> (*Sathya Sai Speaks*, 7, p. 291)

There are certain rules that must be observed while starting the prayer to God, who is the ocean of infinite mercy and compassion. He is as near to us as we are to him; and the conscious praying mind establishes itself on the same wavelength and opens up direct communion with God.

At the very outset, we must practise the habit of regular prayer at a regular time and place, for prayer gives us an additional advantage, for it helps us concentrate and reach a state of calm, all passions spent. However, when through regular prayers we find out that God is omnipresent and we can address him at any time and at any place, we can pray to him no matter where we are, for the prayer will reach him. Baba has advised:

> It is our duty to ask God. Words must be said and the words

must correspond to the thought. The thought must be put into a true word. It is true enough that the divinity knows all, but he requires that the true word be said. The mother knows that to maintain life, the child requires food, but milk is given when the child asks for it.

(*Conversations*, p. 42)

It is imperative for us to know what we should pray for:

Our devotion and prayer to God should not be for the sole purpose of obtaining something, or fulfilling some desire of ours. This should be for the sake of the *Atma* (inner divinity) and for the sake of becoming one with the Lord and for the sake of getting the bliss that one can get by being close to the Lord.

(*Summer Showers*, 1974, p. 176)

However, there is no absolute formula about the choice of one's prayer. Generally speaking, prayer for the removal of obstacles on the spiritual path has a greater chance of being answered than those that relate to personal ambitions and desires, miraculous cures and worldly acquisitions. In any case, it is always necessary to put absolute trust in God. He takes proper care of our needs without being asked for, when we try to live a good life and dedicate all our thought and actions to him. Since the Lord is our eternal parent, he grants us the boons beneficial for us. In the words of Sathya Sai Baba,

If a *bhaktha* (devotee) has dedicated his all—body, mind and existence—to the Lord, the Lord will himself look after everything, for he will always be with the *bhaktha*. Under such conditions, there is no need for prayer. But have you so dedicated and surrendered yourself to the Lord?

(*Prasanthi Vahini*, p. 14)

Sathya Sai Baba has often stated that in the present age, *Namasmaran* or the remembrance of the name and form of the Lord is enough unlike in the other ages where other modes of spiritual exercises were practised. In the words of Sai Baba,

The present age is described in the *Sastras* (sacred texts) as very conducive to liberation. In the past ages religious

> practice was prescribed as the means; the *Kali* age in which you are requires only *namasmaran* (remembrance of the name of the Lord) to win liberation.
>
> (*Sathya Sai Speaks,* 4, p. 106)

But Baba states the crux of the problem when he says,

> *Namasmaran* is the best means but you do not really believe that it can cure or save you: that is the tragedy. People only believe in the efficacy of costly, brightly packaged, widely published drugs; the simple, easily available remedy which is in everybody's dooryard is ignored as useless.
>
> (*Sathya Sai Speaks,* pp. 105-06)

Thus, the name of the Lord, if remembered with sincerity and feeling, enables us to win God's grace and reach our goal. The name of the Lord is like a lantern in the forest wilderness of the world. It is the easiest and the most practical type of *sadhana* for everyone. As Jonathan Roof has wisely remarked,

> We may not command the spiritual power to rise in meditation to formless bliss. We may not possess the devotional heart that allows us to float in the warmth of the divine sea. We may be unable to perform the dedicated service that unfetters the chains of our actions. But if we hold fast to the name of God, we can still achieve fulfilment.
>
> Constant remembrance of the name is complete spiritual discipline; it fosters the virtues of devotion, patience and faith. The practice grants us strength and confidence to travel the spiritual path to its conclusion. In time it can endow us with God-realization. Then we will know that the God we worship is within us, in our own hearts, ever present and joyful.
>
> (Jonathan Roof, *Pathways to God,* p. 75)

No wonder that

> The name is enough to give you all the results of every type of *sadhana* (spiritual discipline).
>
> (*Sathya Sai Speaks,* 3, p. 15)

Satsang or keeping spiritual company with the holy has

always been the preoccupation of all those who seek enlightenment. They simply want to bask in the atmosphere of light and love which the association with the saintly and the holy provides them. On the contrary, unwholesome company washes us away on the dark current of grief, self-indulgence and sin. As Sathya Sai Baba has put it,

> The easiest and most fruitful method of keeping yourself free from dust and rust is *satsang* (good company). The company of the good and Godly will slowly and surely chasten and cleanse the persons prone to staying away from the straight path towards self-realization.
>
> (*Sathya Sai Speaks*, 9, p. 223)

That is why in spiritual life, one must vicariously cling to the company of the good and noble persons set on the pilgrimage on the Godward path. Good company is desirable and important both for the advanced spiritual seeker as well as the new-comer. Baba asks us to

> Join *Satsang,* the company of the godly. Just as the tame elephants surround the wild tusker and rope him and bind him hand and foot, and immobilize him before taming him, the spiritually minded will bring the doubter around.
>
> (*Sathya Sai Speaks*, 2, p. 187)

The benefits of *satsang* are immense. It can not only generate tremendous spiritual energy but also inspire us to turn Godward and make our task of achieving liberation easier. It can grant us a vision of our destination and provide a model for our journey.

While considering the different voices of our calling, we cannot afford to overlook song or *bhajan* which is the very quintessence of our aspiration and apprehension of the divine. Song is the tonic for the weary traveller; it lightens our souls and fills us with the taste of heaven.

Spiritual music is the universal language of the heart; it is the truest and the most resonant voice of our calling, or *atmanivedana.*

Whereas everyone can express his soulful ardour, devotion and yearning through the medium of the beautiful songs or *bhajans* composed by eminent devotional poets, for the poet it is the outpouring of the sweetest elixir of the soul. We have the example of the medieval lyricists, the Sufi poets and of the seventeenth century Metaphysical poets who have all excelled in composing the greatest religious poetry. In India, the *bhajans* composed by Mira, Surdas and Tulsidas have been set to music and are household *bhajans* sung by the common man. Group singing has many more advantages than the singing of *bhajans* in solo. *Bhajan* can be indubitably great poetry and can instantly move the hearts of the listeners and promote the atmosphere of sanctity, love and self-surrender. The *bhajans* composed by Mira and sung by M.S. Subulaxmi, the renowned South Indian singer, leave the listeners almost spell-bound. The same M.S. Subulaxmi sings the Sai *bhajans* in her melodious and incantatory voice during the birthday festival of Sri Sathya Sai Baba and then we come to realize what great poetry and great music can do. The ecstasy is total and all-inclusive; the greatest impact of great poetry and great music sung in chorus can create a lasting effect, that of elemental joy and tranquillity. Love and devotion well up spontaneously in the heart. Remembrance of God becomes constant and steady. When we sing in devotion, joy is likely to remain in our hearts all day long. The effort results in the expansion of our consciousness and consequent transformation of our hearts. God, the almighty is no longer afar or abstract or unreachable. He becomes our kin and we are blessed by the effulgence of his presence. It may not be wrong to say that song or *bhajan* is the most emphatic and effective voice of our calling. Sathya Sai Baba has said in his inimitable style:

> You must pass your days in song. Let your whole life be a *bhajan*. Believe that God is everywhere at all times and derive strength, comfort and joy, singing in your heart in his presence the glory of God. Let melody and harmony surge up from your hearts and let all take delight in the love you express through that song.
>
> (*Sathya Sai Speaks,* 10, p. 75)

The joy which we derive from song helps to sustain and encourage us on the path. It binds us to the Lord and attracts his grace. At the same time, God derives joy from our joy. The bliss of song binds us to him as few other practices can. Baba himself admits:

> The *ananda* (bliss) that I derive from *bhajan* I do not get from anything else.
>
> (*Sathya Sai Speaks*, 8, p. 48)

That is the reason why Swami manifests his presence mysteriously wherever his glory is sung. At Prasanthi Nilayam almost always at the end of his discourse, Swami makes it a point to sing a few *bhajans* which evoke the feeling of elevation and ecstasy to the assembled devotees. And that is perhaps the reason why the pink and blue halo on the face of Swami increases, extending to the limitless sky and the distant facade of the horizons, a fact that has been noted by Professor Varoneshky of Arizona University and by many a discerning devotee.

Harmony and devotion must ultimately be the result of a good song meeting. All who participate must work together with tolerance and the knowledge that the Lord himself is present. Baba says:

> Wherever my *bhakthas* sing my name I am present there.
>
> (*Sanatana Sarathi*, June 1984, p. 161)

Apart from the different ways of remembering and calling the Lord there are a few others which may be said to be of seminal importance. However, these are not so easy to follow because they involve long and continuous *sadhana* costing not less than everything. Some of these also presuppose a native, inborn quality, an attitude of the mind and natural tendencies that come from one's inheritance and as rewards for good works done in one's past lives. In the remaining portion of this chapter, we shall discuss the two important modes of spiritual *sadhana*, meditation and fostering of devotion for the eternal Absolute. While meditation is something that can be practised by all of us, the flower of devotion for the Lord can only blossom in the heart that is saturated with love.

Meditation means absorption in God for the purposes of attaining enlightenment and bliss. Moreover, meditation is not and can never be a conscious process. So long as one knows that he is meditating, he is not really meditating. Since meditation is a mystique, in practising meditation, the mind stops and one gets totally immersed in God. For the spiritual aspirant, meditation is the inner contemplation. With time, meditation develops true understanding of the self and thereby leads to the blissful merger with God. Although meditation is not actually a voice of one's calling or supplication to the Divine, it does establish a sense of oneness with God.

Sai Baba has described as the most universal the light meditation. Baba suggests that a small lamp or candle may be used which may help the meditator to visualize the flame of light and truth. This flame is pictured between the eyebrows as the light of wisdom; from there it is brought on to the heart, and visualised as a lotus of love blooming petal by petal. As the light grows, it purifies all the senses and impulses, taking all in the light of divine love. Over time, the meditation purifies the individual's thoughts and actions, making him or her fit for realization of divinity.

Sathya Sai Baba has said:

> In real *dhyana*, you soon get over the consciousness that you are doing *dhyana*. In fact, every moment in life must be utilized for *dhyana*. That is the best way to live. When you sweep your rooms clean tell yourselves that your hearts too have to be swept likewise. When you cut vegetables, you feel that lust and greed too have to be cut into pieces. When you press *chapatis* wider and wider, desire in addition that your love take in wider and wider circles and expand even into the regions of strangers and foes.
>
> (*Sathya Sai Speaks*, 6, p. 298)

And finally, Sathya Sai Baba declares:

> By means of *dhyana* you can realize that I am the resident in all hearts, the urge, the motive, the guide, the goal. Yearn for that vision, that awareness, and make it your priceless possession.
>
> (*Sathya Sai Speaks*, 7, pp. 473-74)

Sathya Sai Baba has explained the full significance of light or the flame in meditation. In answer to a question put by a western devotee Baba has stated:

> Why a light? From the sand, if one takes it will be depleted, from the water tank, if each one takes, the tank will go dry. But a thousand people can take the flame of one candle to light their candles and the flame is in no way diminished. Light a lamp or a candle. Gaze straight ahead at the flame. Then take the candle flame, the *jyoti* into your heart and see it in the midst of the petals of the heart. Watch the petals of the heart unfold and see the light illumine the heart. Bad feelings cannot remain. Then move the flame into the hands and they can no longer do dark deeds. In turn, move the flame in like fashion to the eyes and ears so they may henceforth take only bright and pure sensations. Then move the light outward and into your friends, relatives and enemies, and then into animals, birds and other objects so that all are illumined by the same light. Christ said, 'All are one, be alike to everyone.' In this way you will no longer be limited to the body, but will expand throughout the universe. The world which is now so big, will become very small. To expand beyond self and to see that your light is the light of the universe is liberation. Liberation is not different from this.
>
> (*Conversations*, p. 186)

This kind of pointed meditation ensures expansion of the self beyond desire to an infinity of love and provides elemental bliss and serenity that is the sure mark of illumination. Meditation, thus, is the most useful and effective way of calling the Divine.

Total and unqualified surrender to the divine will and selfless service to the suffering humanity are the other two vital factors which make the voice of the aspirant heard by God. The point to be noted here is: what do we actually surrender to God? What do we have which we can offer to him? Since he is the master of the creation, every sentient object of this shadow world is already his. The flower that we offer to him in worship or the service that we offer him are all his. So, what we surrender to him is our acceptance of his divine will, the renunciation of the illusion of our separateness from him and our self-effacement and abandonment of our ego. We must perform actions without desire for the fruits of action, surrendering everything to God. In a different sense, what we actually surrender to God is our agonizing feeling of dualism. In the real sense of the term, surrender to a higher power is tantamount to surrender to oneself, to the *Atma* or the inner divinity enthroned in our hearts. In the words of Sai Baba,

> Surrendering to the Lord is surrendering all thoughts and actions, not wishing for the fruits of the action, not doing the action to gain its fruit, but doing the action because it is one's duty. The act is dedicated to the Lord, and the results, therefore, are borne by the Lord.
>
> (*Conversations*, pp. 13-14)

Such a surrender envisages full faith and complete reliance on God as the doer of all deeds:

> Rely on the Lord and accept whatever is your lot. He is in you, with you. He knows what to give and when. He is full of *Prema* (love).
>
> (*Sathya Sai Speaks*, 6, p. 176)

The path of total surrender to the will of the Lord is the safest one and is sure to produce the desired result. The only condition is that the surrender should be true and complete. Baba emphatically declares:

> Surrender to me only. When the surrender is complete and all acts, words and thoughts are dedicated to the Lord along with all their consequences then he has promised that he will free you from sin and sorrow.
>
> (*Sathya Sai Speaks*, 5, p. 54)

The practice of complete and unqualified spiritual surrender is a spiritual exercise of a very high order. It costs not less than everything. The greatest obstacle to this is our ego, the big 'I' which takes pride in its supremacy over everything and queers the pitch of our surrender. It is necessary, therefore, to cross the 'I'.

Service to suffering and the afflicted is another sure way of earning the grace of the Lord. Service to the society and the community is our obligatory duty since we are part of the society and the community. In fact, we are an integral part of the whole community of mankind. If we do not serve God in the form of our unfortunate brothers and sisters, how can we serve God or experience a sense of oneness with the divine father? We have to work incessantly for the brotherhood of man and the fatherhood of God. In all important world religions, as well as the tenets of humanism, there is great stress on service to the poor, needy, diseased and afflicted. It is said that service to mankind is service to God. The motivating force for undertaking selfless service to our unfortunate brothers and sisters is, of course, our love and compassion and the realization that all are the important components of the same divinity that presides over the destiny of all mankind. In this sense, the act of serving others becomes a spiritual discipline which engenders spiritual joy and satisfaction to the server. It promotes the awareness within us in no uncertain terms that we are in others; others' suffering is our suffering and the joy of the others is our joy. Such a feeling is unique and entirely salutary; it broadens our vision and widens our compassion. As Baba has rightly pointed out,

> If the individual is deluded into believing that he is serving others then woe be to him, for there is no other at all. All are one; one man's sorrow is everyone's sorrow. The fundamental flaw is the ignorance of man. If only he was wise, he would have known that all individuals are waves on the surface of the self-same ocean.
>
> (*Sathya Sai Speaks,* 3, p. 62)

Thus service can develop into a highly beneficial spiritual discipline and with constant practice it becomes indispensable and essential trait of our very nature. Furthermore, the joy we derive from selfless service blossoms into detachment. When we serve God in others, we find that God is resident in our own hearts. The desire for selfish gains vanishes and we experience lasting happiness. As Baba has said,

> One cannot cross the ocean of this cycle of births and deaths

> by visiting many sacred places, nor one can do it by performing *japa* or studying *Sastras* (holy books). It is only possible to do so by performing *Sewa* or service.
>
> (*Summer Showers*, 1973, p. 75)

The obvious lesson is that service to suffering humanity enables us to grow spiritually by expressing our love in action. Thus, we should be grateful to those who offer us opportunity to serve them and have thus opened for us the glimpse of the celestial city where God resides.

Finally, the supreme motivation for our resonant call and anguished cry is what we call our devotion to the Lord. Devotion is the latent quality in the heart of man that has come into his proud possession mainly on account of his noble and virtuous antecedents in his former life. As we know, according to the doctrine of *karma* we reap what we have sown in our past lives: there is no escape from the consequence of *karma*. But devotion to God removes the bad effects of *karma*. The good, virtuous and noble deeds done in the past lives influence our *prarabdha* (earned destiny) and have the capacity to offset the adverse effect of such *karma*. It is in this sense that devotion, whole-hearted devotion to the Lord, burns away all our sins and shortcomings and makes us a vessel for the blessings of the Lord now and forever more.

In the words of Jonathan Roof,

> Devotion is a mystery of the heart. No amount of argument can persuade us to feel devotion towards the Lord, for it is the bond between the creator and the created which surpasses our rational understanding. Perhaps, it is our nature to feel and express devotion. It may result from lifetimes of spiritual striving. Actually devotion is comprised of many feelings, emotions and thoughts. It includes gratitude, reverence, adoration, love, thanksgiving, even fear of sin, but ultimately all descriptions must fail. For, in truth, devotion is only experienced by the *bhaktha* as the *bhaktha* is understood only by the Lord.
>
> The spiritual path of devotion to God is called in the Hindu religious texts as *bhakthi marg;* the other paths are the way of selfless action (*karma yoga*) and the way of knowledge and

> wisdom (*jnana yoga*). Each of these paths is difficult to practice as each demands the reduction and annihilation of the ego to be able to merge with the divine principle. However, in the present age, *bhakthi marg* or the way of devotion is the easiest to practice. The *bhakthi* devotee seeks to realize God by reducing ego to nothing. When our ego disappears, only God is left. Devotion promotes humility and surrender to divine will.
>
> (Jonathan Roof, *Pathways to God*, p. 189)

Sai Baba has made this point very clear when he dwells on the excellence of the devotional path. He says:

> *Bhakthi* is the through carriage. Though it may be detached from one train and connected to another, if you get into it, you need not worry; so long as you stick to your place, It is bound to take you to your destination.
>
> (*Sathya Sai Speaks*, 3, p. 134)

Fervent devotion to the Lord is the first step to the spiritual ladder, always be tempered with duty and discipline. Baba's injunction to each one of us is:

> Imbibe the ideals of duty, devotion and discipline. Devotion must be tested in the crucible of discipline. It must be directed on the lines of duty.
>
> (*Sathya Sai Speaks*, 9, p. 220)

Devotion is a full-time endeavour. It consists in seeing divinity in everyone and in all places. Its aim not only is self-transformation but also God realization.

> When grief overtakes you, you run to God...when joy is restored you throw him overboard. *Bhakthi* is not temporary salve. It is unbroken contemplation of God without any interposing thought or feeling.
>
> (*Geeta Vahini*, p. 223)

How do we start on the path of devotion towards God? There is no formula absolute for such a beginning. It depends largely on the temperament and sensibility of the aspirant. If his heart is full of love, universal love, he sets off on his journey pretty soon and with extreme confidence. Because he loves God already, the Lord himself takes the full responsibility and becomes his mentor and guide.

The devotee establishes his own particular and favourite relationship with God. No single relation for all is either necessary or desirable.

One person may assume the attitude of a child towards the parent; another may love God as a friend or companion; yet another like Mira may love God as a spouse or a bridegroom. What is of the greatest significance is the intensity of that love, the sanction of the weight of feeling. All forms of relationship is accepted by God so long as the craving and the yearning arise from the very core of the heart. So, we come to the conclusion that there are different modes of calling the divine master and if we endeavour to please the Lord and to appropriate him through coronets and garlands of deep devotion and love, God is bound to listen to us and our prayers are answered immediately. Baba has said that one should yearn for him and lead a life of constant devotion, ardour and self-surrender. The crux of the problem is the steady, constant and continual devotion.

> God is ignored in sunshine; he is wanted only when there is night. Devotion must persist and flourish, unaffected by time, place and circumstance.
>
> (*Sathya Sai Speaks*, 9, p. 221)

The Lord guides and protects us when we surrender to his will. To win grace, however, we must immerse ourselves in God and strive to do his will.

> It is God's word that if you have devotion in God, he will look after all your future. He will look after all the welfare that is due to you.
>
> (*Summer Showers*, 1972, p. 105)

The culmination of full-time devotion is seeing God in all things. Then, all events and beings are seen in the light of God. Nothing is separate from God, for when we are filled with God, we see only God. Then we know beyond doubt that we have reached the summit of the practice. We experience joy and peace beyond measure. Sai Baba has said the last word about *bhakthi* which is the consummation of our love for the eternal Absolute who draws all of us like a magnet unto him. Baba says:

> *Bhakthi* is the state of mind in which one has no separate existence apart from God. His very breath is God, his every act is God, for God; his thoughts are of God; his words are uttered by God, about God. For like the fish which can only live in water man can only live in God—in peace and happiness.
>
> (*Sathya Sai Speaks*, 6, p. 119)

With this submission about the supreme and paramount value of devotion as the pitch and the volume of our supplication to the Divine, we again return to the glorious and august presence of Sathya Sai Baba in our midst who symbolizes the Eternal Absolute and the Ultimate Reality, the reservoir and fountainhead of all love, power and glory. He is a Ray from the Supreme to take humanity to the life eternal and to offer us liberation from the recurrent and painful cycle of death and birth. It is indeed our duty to take full advantage of his divine presence. All we need to do is to follow the guidelines given by him for living up to the exacting standards set by him. And the rest is not our business. The loving merciful Lord who is spreading the splendour of his redemptive love all round through every nook and corner of the world, will see to it that we reach our destination and be worthy of his love now and forever more.

Sathya Sai Baba, like Krishna and Jesus Christ, is the path, the way and the pilgrim, the means and the goal. Sai Baba says that love is his form and that consciousness expands by and through the fostering, cultivation and expansion of love. Teaching love by love for love and through acts of love, unconditional, selfless love the Avatar gives the faith, strength and inspiration to reach for heaven and to that glorious unitary state beyond. Baba has penned the following inspiring message to all the spiritual aspirants who strive to reach that blessed state of Being, Awareness and Bliss:

> Let the different faiths exist. Let them flourish. Let the glory of God be sung in all languages and a variety of tunes. This should be the ideal: respect the differences between the faiths,

and recognize them as valid as far as they do not extinguish the flame of unity. I have not come to speak on behalf of any particular religion. I have not come on a mission of publicity for any sect or creed nor have I come to collect followers for any doctrine. I have come to tell you of this universal, unitary path, this path of love, this duty of love, this obligation to love...

The totality of divine energy has come into humanity as Sathya Sai—to go to each and everyone to wake up the slumbering divinity of every human being. Even if in your sleepiness or in your weakness for sleep, you growl, grumble or groan, kick, criticise, quarrel or cry, I will not forsake you. I will not let your divinity to go to sleep. Mother never forsakes the child she carries or lets the child fall down, even if the child works out its resentment and anger on her. I have come to help, to accompany and to carry you. I can never forsake you, I will never fail in my duty to my children — and I shall be very grateful to each child of mine who helps my task...

Wake up my children. Wake up to the dawn of knowledge; wake up to your divine duties, wake up to your divine rights and wake up to your divine reality.

(Sathya Sai Baba)

The central basic assumption in this study, which has now been reiterated and stated precisely and tangibly with enough supportive evidence, is that Sai Baba is a Ray from the Supreme. He is a divine power station. As Professor Gokak has beautifully described:

...But these laws of Nature can be transcended whenever a ray direct from the Supreme penetrates the universe. This ray is power, will, thought and feeling combined in a solar flash. The Word which is at the very root of Creation, is a complex seed—symphony of Truth, Beauty, Goodness, Love, Delight and Power...When does the ray descend? As the Gita says, whenever righteousness is at a low ebb and the unrighteous ride on the crest of the wave, the Ray takes human form to establish the reign of Truth again, to protect the good and to punish the wicked.

(V.K. Gokak, *Sai Baba: Man and Avatar*, p. 12)

The present moment of history is precisely a time of crisis when mankind is poised precariously at the very brink of a precipice and a conflagration, a veritable *pralaya* seems to be imminent, the advent of an *Avatar* was very much anticipated. The saints and sages prayed and the Eternal Absolute, the Supreme Brahman incarnated on earth as Sai Baba. He has been continuing his mission and with the incessant labours of an *Avatar* has already cleared many of the mists that had darkened not only the scenario of the world but also the outlook and attitude of man. By his insistence on the age-old verities of truth, love, righteousness, peace and non-violence and by the instrument of the magical redemptive power of love, he has taken us out of the black pall surrounding us and we now stand on the summit of the hill from where we can visualize the resplendent minarets of that celestial city which is our true home. Mankind has, thus, experienced the vision of the divine and is engaged in the spiritual *sadhana* that would take the pilgrim to his destination.

As a fitting sequel to this, our last chapter, we would like to quote from Howard Murphet's wonderful book *Where the Road Ends* the portion that relates the exciting experience of Collin Best, a young technician of Sydney, Australia who sensed the utter emptiness of the existential encounter and took recourse to the techniques of meditation and astral projection or travel outside the body. This is how Howard Murphet describes the momentous experience of Collin Best:

> Then one day, after about eight months, he made an unexpected breakthrough in astral projection. Finding himself outside his physical body, he was so alarmed that he went straight back to it. But he persisted, going a little further each time, until eventually he travelled right around the world... It was eight O'clock in the evening in the year 1972, he told me, when he made a desperate effort to breach the solid wall of the mind. He sat cross-legged on the floor in front of a full-length mirror and concentrated on the point between his two eyes. For twenty minutes nothing at all happened. Then

several strange things happened. The first was the production of copious saliva from his mouth. When this stopped, tears began to run down his cheeks, and after that came a tingling in his scalp...the fourth was that his image in the mirror completely disappeared and a greyness took its place. A strange voice near him asked, 'What do you want to happen next?'

Somewhat startled, Collin asked, 'Who are you?'

'A friend.'

'What is your name?'

'Peter.'

'Oh!' said Collin who had been brought up as a Christian. 'Peter, the fisherman?'

'No,' the voice replied. 'He is on a different plane.'

...Something prompted Collin to ask if there was anybody on earth today who was as great as, or greater than, Jesus Christ?

'Yes,' Peter replied, 'There is one who is greater.'

'What is his name?'

'I cannot tell you.'

'Well, where is he?'

'I cannot tell you that either.'

'Why?'

'Because it's your search.'

'Well, when will I find this one?'

'In fifteen years' time.'

Collin could think of nothing else but this one living being on earth greater than Jesus. He could not wait fifteen years. He must leave his body and find this great one wherever he was on earth. So leaving his physical body sitting cross-legged before a mirror, he was over to India in a flash hovering over the country and looking down from his astral body...He thought undoubtedly, this great one for whom he was searching, must be surrounded by a bright light. So, soaring slowly in his astral body above India, he concentrated on finding this bright light...It was no longer before he spotted it outshining the pale street lights...he went straight towards the light and says that within the time of a heart-beat, he was there standing before what looked to him like a temple...He says, 'In front of me, sitting on a stage, was a small man, dressed in a red-orange robe with a mop of fuzzy hair...'

Towards the end of his fifteen years' wait, Collin met a girl named Sue who had similar interests to his own.

...One day Collin wanted a certain book and Sue told him that he could find it in a certain bookstall in Sydney. Obtaining the book, he took home and here is what happened in his own words: 'I turned a few pages and there, lo and behold, was a photo of the little fuzzy headed figure sitting in a chair. My heart almost stopped. But now I knew his name and address.'

...Within a very short time, Collin was at Prasanthi Nilayam sitting at the feet of Sathya Sai Baba. It was now 1987, just fifteen years after he had tried in vain to come to the feet of the great one.

(*Where the Road Ends*, pp. 209-10)

Stranger is the story of Klaus Remme, who was told by a German doctor: 'When you are sixty years old, you will look into the eyes of God. Now prepare yourself by living a good life.' This was prophesied forty-two years before Klaus Remme actually sat on the *darshan* line at Prasanthi Nilayam and looked into the eyes of Swami. Earlier, he had seen in a dream vision that Swami held his face in both hands and said, 'My love for you is eternal.' Klaus Remme responded, 'I love you, too.'

(Murphet, *op. cit.*, p. 212)

On this note, triumphant note, we would like to close the chapter knowing full well that in spiritual realm, what we call the end is often the beginning of an hope that the love and blessings of Sai Baba will be our safe guide and lighthouse to cross the ocean of the *samsara*.